To Ka...   ...rts

                    and flip-flops

Best wishes

PAJohn.

Terry Johnson

Flying cats
and flip-flops

Surviving A
Notorious
African Prison

PAUL JOHNSON

Interior Design and Layout by *www.wordzworth.com*
First Published in Great Britain in 2013
By Noproblempublishing Ltd

ISBN 978-0-9575097-0-2 Paperback
ISBN 978-0-9575097-1-9 E Book

This work is classified as non-fiction. It is a memoir and such reflects that as
told by the author and is a recollection of experiences over a specified period
of time. Certain names, places and identifying characteristics have been
changed to ensure anonymity. Additionally some individuals are composite.
Dialogue and events have been recreated from memory, and, in some cases,
have been compressed to convey the substance of what was said
or what occurred.

A CIP catalogue record for this title is available from the British Library

Acknowledgements

All my love to three beautiful ladies in my life.

To my wife and daughters. X.

You were my eyes.

Your love support and devotion will always be remembered as I came to terms with losing my sight.

Those weekly trips to London, battling the crowds on the underground my arm linked in yours, white stick in hand, as we made our way to Moorfields Eye Hospital.

That time we got onto a busy train, upgraded free of charge to first class (There are some perks) and telling me not to order too much from the coffee and sweet trolley- but it was no good: I could hear the rattle and vibration of that trolley getting nearer every time. I could sense your embarrassment as we left our seats at Paddington leaving behind a mountain of sweet wrappers and empty cups.

Having my sight taken was without doubt the toughest thing I've ever experienced and having you and the girls with me gave me hope, kept me positive and kept me laughing. All three of you got me through it and I love you all very much.

Love and kisses for my sister in law and her old flat, AKA Hotel Bracey.

To my bro and gorgeous sis in law in Canada for our amazing post operation holiday of a lifetime in B.C.

To Stephen Simonds and Aaron Kwok - Thanks for being there when I needed you both.

A special thank you also goes to the miracle workers at Moorfields, including Mr Barton (Head of Glaucoma) who gave me some sight back in my right eye, giving me a new lease of life and made writing this book all the more possible.

Contents

Preface

It was eight years since we last spoke and I took a phone call at work from the British embassy in Nairobi. Eight years is a long time to go without speaking to your dad.

"Your father is in a Kenyan prison, he's in very poor health and may not make it through," said Nigel, one of the embassy managers.

I had more or less blocked the old man out. He had his life and I had mine, but when I heard the news he could die in an African prison, any bitter feelings about my relationship with him melted away. My first reaction was to get over there and see him, so I left work early that day, got to the clinic, had the jabs and looked at available flights to Kenya.

"Don't come over here, it's a dangerous place." Nigel reiterated my dad's feelings on the subject of me going over. I had my own family to think of and agreed not to go; instead, Nigel kept me informed by email throughout his sentence.

When he came home events in my life changed dramatically. I lost my sight. A detached retina from a car accident left me instantly blinded in my left eye, and three different conditions in my right left me seeing dark shadows.

I got back in touch with my dad who was shocked to see me with my new white stick, and my wife dropped me to his place for our weekly get together and we'd sit outside and I'd listen to his stories, each one more incredible than the last as he slowly began to fill in the gaps of the past eight years.

I was awaiting an operation to at least save some of the sight in my right eye and made a promise to my dad. When I got my sight back I would write his book. On June 17th 2010, the wonderful staff and surgeons at Moorfields Eye Hospital in London saved the sight in my right eye and I've been writing his story ever since.

Flying Cats and Flip Flops is a surreal incredible true-life African experience, told in my father's words. I hope you enjoy it as much I did.

1. A Warm Welcome

"God, it's good to hear your voice." It was good hearing his too. I tried calling him from the airport but it just went straight to answer phone. I hate those bloody things, so I just rang off and tried him again at Paddington. He asked me what time I got in. I wasn't sure on the exact time but I let him do the talking, and he brought me bang up to date: where he'd been, what he'd been up to. He waffled on a bit but it was a comfort to hear his chirpy south west accent. I didn't say a lot and might not have sounded like the old Terry, so it was his way of putting me at ease.

My next thought was for my ticket. I panicked, tilting my head to one side, cradling the phone to free up both hands so I could empty the crap out of my pockets onto the shelf. Tissues, a cheap plastic lighter, a few coins and a folded five-shilling note. I even looked down, checking the floor space around me, patting the back pockets of my trousers.

"Terry, you still there?" I eventually found it in my shirt pocket. "What time d'you get in?"

"Shit."

I stepped out, away from the phone as far as the tightened cord would let me so I could get a proper look at the departures board and panicked again. Must have got the trains mixed up and had less than three minutes to get my train.

"Look, don't worry, just get on the train, we'll find out when it gets in and we'll be there for you, ok?"

"Thanks Ted."

I didn't have a seat reservation and by the time I got to platform eight, the train was already rammed with people. A gang of students sat on their luggage at the end of the carriage, blocking the area near

3

the door. I walked towards the toilet and a young lad with a giant backpack strapped to his back moved aside from the door he was blocking and that's where I spent the first forty or so minutes of my journey – sat on the only seat that wasn't reserved – the loo.

The section of frosted glass in the window restricted my view, so to pass time, I sat staring, inspecting the room fittings. It was typical train standard; stainless steel, a hinged seat with a built-in flush button and toilet paper fitted from the wall. A bit different from the bucket on a rope I'd been used to. And that got me thinking of other things I'd missed. Like tea. A nice sugary cup of tea was near the top of my list followed by coffee, especially the smell of it. It was nice not to have to hide away to smoke a cigarette and read a newspaper (a different one from the same one I had read word for word over the last year).

In my time away I'd tried hard not to think too much about home. In fact, I'd made a conscious effort to block out my past and live in the moment. I thought missing England would be a weakness and knew if I was going to get through it all I needed to be strong.

I nodded off and woke again to a jolting, jerking motion as the train slowed up, shuddering its way into Reading station. This was my chance. London commuters emptied out here, and as they did, I nipped out quickly before the train refilled and claimed a table seat by the window.

I'd done this journey many times. My favourite bit is when the train gets to Devon and the track cuts through the rock at Dawlish. You can pick up the scent of the coast and follow the sea wall where the waves roll in, smashing on the beach below. This was a special day for me and I framed the memory in my mind and can still recall it clearly today, eleven years on.

Bright sunshine lit the sea which glistened blue, and there wasn't a cloud in the sky. I was relieved to be back but nervous all the same and tried to imagine Ann's reaction as I turned up unannounced at the door.

I tried ringing her but the line was dead – an unpaid bill was more likely the reason than changing her number.

I left a note five years ago and had not seen her since. This was going to be interesting. Maybe she'd met someone else. Her new bloke answering the door to me, now that would be awkward.

Plymouth station felt familiar, but at the same time, so strange. I stepped onto the platform and walked towards the barriers. It was strange in the sense that this place I had returned to which I knew as home seemed like another planet from where I'd been.

Ted and Rita walked from where they stood on the platform, waving and smiling at me. Rita saw me, opened her arms and waited for a cuddle, then Ted shook my hand wildly. I felt a bit self-conscious at first, the noise and fuss they made, and I wondered if others were watching, but unlike us they all seemed in a rush to get off the platform.

"Good to see you, mate." Rita planted a smacker of a kiss on my cheek while Ted tried grabbing my case. It was a small holdall, not very heavy but he just had the urge to help me. Did I now look that frail?

"Come on, let me carry that."

I swung the case away from him and told him I was fine. We walked away talking and he never gave up snatching at my hand to wrestle the case from me.

When we got to his car a traffic warden stood balanced on the edge of the kerb taking down the registration. Ted shouted and started running, doing his best to get his attention. Strangers looked around before they got into black cabs and the drivers stood at each other's cars chatting, watching the event unfold. Would he get a ticket or could he blag it? I could tell the taxi drivers enjoyed this piece of drama in their day, their attention now on Ted and this warden, waiting for the outcome.

Ted was fully animated now, arms flapping, pacing about on the spot trying his best to convince the warden but this bloke wasn't having any of it. He kept his eyes on the machine in his hand, tapping at it.

He beckoned the warden to walk with him away from us, his voice was quieter now but I still heard certain words involving me so I knew he was using my situation to plead his case. I looked at Rita, laughing. "He hasn't changed." I lit a fag.

"You ok?"

"Yeh, am now."

"Did it drag?"

"What, on the train?"

"No ya fool, in—"

"Nope, only the last two days. I didn't let it drag but the last two days seemed to go on forever."

"You look so thin."

I laughed at the way she came straight out with the questions.

"You hungry?"

"I've been hungry for the last sixteen months."

"No, I mean—"

"I know what you mean, no it's ok, I'm fine."

The conversation dried up so she left me alone to finish my fag and to see how Ted was getting on. I flicked the butt away, kicking the kerb gently with my toe, thinking about what she'd just said, which made me think of Heathrow.

I used the toilets after landing and saw myself in the mirror for the first time in ages. I used a cubicle, came out, pumped soap into both hands at the sink and then looked at myself. Weight loss had shrunk my six-foot broad frame but it was the shock of seeing my face. The last couple of years were etched on it and I just stood there without blinking, watching myself. It was me alright, but much older.

I'd aged ten years. I bent over the sink, moved under the halogens to get a better look, squinting, pulling the loose folds of skin, stretching it over my sunken, gaunt features. My dark tanned face was a road map of new lines and wrinkles.

Ted was now back-slapping the warden, laughing and joking with him like he was his best mate. No ticket, well done Ted.

The chit-chat in the car was trivial although I knew what they wanted to really ask me, but they kept conversation to the subjects of work, the weather and the kids, but they did try and warn me.

"Look Terr, when you see the house you're gonna be shocked. You know how fussy and house-proud she was, well the house is a right state. David's at the house a lot, with his friends but she just stays upstairs and lets him get on with it. She hasn't been seen outside for a year or so." It went quiet for the next five minutes. They sensed I had a lot to take in.

We stopped at traffic lights and Ted tapped at the wheel, waiting for green. Rita leant forward from the back seat, trying to get my attention. "Terry, why don't you take our spare room for a while eh, just until you get sorted?"

I weighed up the offer in silence. "You've been through a lot, Terr, you don't need this right now. Come on, come stay with us."

I could see they meant well but I really needed to face up to whatever waited for me. We pulled up outside the house.

"We're going to stay here, just in case you change your mind, ok?"

The hedge at the bottom of the front garden had been pulled out of shape, flattened, gaping with holes. Makeshift dirt tracks to the house had rubbed away the plants and flowers that I'd once planted which told me no one used the steps anymore.

I knocked and waited.

After a while thinking she wasn't going to answer, I shouted through the letterbox and when she did get to the door she made hard work of the lock, tugging at it, which gave me a moment to look around the garden again.

Black streaks of smoke stained the white paint of the house with lumps of charcoal remains underneath the windowsill. A bike frame stood upside down on its saddle and the wheels from it were hanging in next door's hedge. An empty paint pot full of rusty rainwater by the porch had a collection of floating fag ends.

I turned back to the door, pressing my forehead against the bevelled glass, cupping my hands like binoculars, blocking out the light around me so I could try and see her at least acknowledge me.

"Back door," I said, mouthing it, instructing her through the glass and rattling the door again. "Ann, go to the back door."

I went around the back but could still see her outline through the net curtain, still wrestling the lock.

"Ann, Ann." I rattled the door hard, making next door's dog bark which was enough to draw her attention away from the front door and towards me at the back and when she opened it I could tell straight away something was wrong, drastically wrong. Her blank distant expression looked through me and not a word. Five years away, I was expecting much more than this.

"Come on, you took your bloody time," I said, telling her off with a smile.

She stood looking prehistoric, like a grubby cave dweller. A ball of bushy, tangled dry hair, damaged from years of colour and heated tongs, stuck in a clump to one side of her blotchy face.

"Hello." She tried a smile. Dark stained rings under bloodshot eyes looked at me like I'd come to read the meter. Vacant. She walked away, back towards the stairs leaving me to it, standing with the door wide open. Her nightdress was filthy, nowhere near the white it should have been and as she walked I could see dry, cracked skin around her bare heels, blackened with dirt.

Shit. I forgot.

I raced to the front door, unbolting it and found them still sat in their white Mondeo, parked with hazard lights blinking on the bend half-way on the pavement.

I gave 'em a wave and a thumbs up, and as Ted and Rita pulled away, I stepped back into the house, this time noticing a thick pile of letters in the doorway. One-handed, I scooped as many off the floor as I could which made little difference to the ones left there.

Ann made her way back upstairs, with a lot of effort, lifting, shuffling herself sideways, on each step pulling herself up on the bannister. The top layer of unopened letters was covered in smudged footprints. The ones I started opening were final demands, threatening county court judgements. I squatted down, a position I was more than familiar with and raked the letters with both hands, making one big pile, lifting and squashing them against my chest as I looked around for a place to put them.

Ann's breathing got louder as she reached the dog leg part of the stairs and was now shuffling on the spot to get near the bannister again to make the last few steps.

I walked around in disbelief. No exaggeration, the place looked and smelt like a fucking landfill site. The condition of the house matched Ann's state of mind and appearance – the place reeked of stale smoke and putrid food.

My shoes glued to the sticky Lino floor in the kitchen as I walked, lifting, peeling my shoes off it as I went. It looked like every piece of crockery,cutlery and utensil we owned had been used. Different sized pots and pans, plates, dishes and cups were balanced high on each other, stained with different shades of food and furry green mould like an art exhibit.

I opened windows and kept both doors wide open, hoping the air sweeping through the house would take the stench away.

I followed the smell of food which seemed to get stronger upstairs. I was right about the landfill site. The back bedroom was being used as one. Black bin bags of rubbish stacked high, some split with rotten food squashed into the carpet and a good supply of empty tins, mostly Campbell's meatballs tins and packets of Smash dried potato mash, which gave me an idea of what Ann had been living on. The erected tea-stained ironing board was now a table, with a mug rack and a chipped discoloured Disney Pocahontas mug, which she'd had for years.

The kettle, with its cord stretched tight to a socket on the other wall, was ready to drop off the edge of the board at any moment. The blinds were rolled half-way and hung unevenly in the window, one end sloping and a half-filled container of milk sat on the sill with a trail of used, squashed teabags which marked the window sill a ginger colour. I picked the milk up, shaking it, unsettling the block of slush that was in the bottom.

I could hear Ann stirring, and thinking she was awake, I peered back into the room and could see the lump in the duvet move. I waited until she was still again, then carried on my tour.

All this time away, no reaction then back to sleep. I couldn't believe it. I stepped quietly, looking around the room while she slept. Her side of the divan bed was burnt – scorched with brown patches and the curtains along with the floorboards were littered with burn holes.

I'd seen enough. I'd lived in shit for the past sixteen months and I wasn't expecting the same at home. I mooched around the house, uncovering more filth and mess. 'David comes over and brings all his friends to the house, she just stays upstairs and leaves them to virtually run the house.'

David was Ann's son. Thirty-five years old with a child's mind, he'd spent all his life under care supervision and used to visit us once a month and that was enough. He needed psychosis drugs such as Largactil to slow him down but he was still a handful.

I knew my news had travelled fast when I went down the shop. People I knew didn't speak and no-one seemed to have much time for me. The shop was re-branded, redesigned with a new layout but the staff were more or less the same. They all knew me and I even recognised some customers in the queue but no-one spoke. Now Sheila used to be a good laugh, I even used to flirt with her but today she did just enough to be polite and kept her distance. I'd stuffed every type of cleaning product in my shopping trolley and she started scanning each one.

Then I heard my name. I looked around and could see Martin, the shop owner, coming out from behind the glass post office screen. He walked towards me with paper in his hand. "Terry," he said, greeting me with a nod, more of an acknowledgement than anything else. "Look, I know you've been away, but we've got an issue with Ann."

Oh here we go. "She's had papers delivered about a year ago now and she hasn't paid her bill. I even went to the house to speak to her but she denies ever having had them. She got very abusive in the end. " He shuffled through the receipts in his hands.

"How much?"

"Thirty-eight pounds, fifty pence."

I handed him the last twenty quid the embassy gave me and told him I'd pay back every last penny.

I got back to the house and got to work; clearing, scrubbing and polishing every inch of that house. It took about two weeks to get the house and garden clean again. I used the outside drain to empty bucket after bucket of filthy water and was on a mission to clean and de-clutter the house.

I emptied all the kitchen drawers, clearing stuff out and slowly replacing it with new, mostly from the Pound shop, cheap, but more importantly, it was new and clean.

The next few weeks my phone was busy – all related to a common theme. Ann had been busy again with catalogues and credit cards.

I got around to opening all the letters and the total amount of debt came to just under £17,000 and the bills carried on coming. I wondered how or what she could have spent that amount of money on and then I opened all the cupboards including the storage shed outside, and found out. Most of it was unopened and still packaged in the original boxes. Toys, gadgets, jewellery, clothes – even garden furniture – delivered and still in its cellophane wrapping. I put a card ad in the shop window and managed to sell some things before the bailiffs took the rest.

Some of the threatening letters were from credit card companies. She had two credit cards which she'd maxed out and never paid. A person with twenty years of bad debt was given credit cards with a six grand limit – unbelievable! On checking the statements a second time I could see a lot of cash withdrawals. My guess was she was sending David out to the ATMs.

The total outstanding water bill was £1200 and I needed to get this sorted first. I had to walk up to use the phone box because BT had cut our phone off and we needed £400 to get it reconnected. I phoned South West Water and they told me the matter had been taken to court. I agreed to pay £60 over my monthly bill.

I'd closed my bank account a few years back so they sent me a card which I took to the post office to make my payments on a weekly basis. I claimed both Disability and Carers Allowance but had so much to pay back each month to different companies, it left me with next to nothing.

No bank account and no direct debits, I organised myself from a calendar on the wall.

I monitored the days I needed to pay certain bills, how much I had to pay, and I wrote the remaining balance at the start of each month.

That first day when she did eventually wake, I walked into the room and realised she hadn't got up once to use the loo. I prompted this and woke her up. "Come on, let's get you to toilet." She moaned at me like a sleepy, irritated child.

The smell came from her as I peeled the duvet back and could see the grubby base sheet as she got up. She was filthy.

I undressed her and noticed blotchy red patches all over her right leg and both ankles.

I eventually found out from my neighbour what had happened.

"It was a few months back, I was watching telly and I heard a loud scream outside and rushed to my door," said Barbara who lives on the corner near the house. Ann stood on the pavement in her nightdress in front of her house screaming, she was holding her leg in pain so she took her to hospital and they treated her burns. Apparently she dropped a kettle of boiling water over herself. My mind went straight to the landfill site and the kettle she kept on the edge of the ironing board.

I sat her on the toilet and told her to wait there while I stripped the bedding. We had no shower so I stood her in the bath and flanneled her with warm water and soap. Dirty water ran away as I scrubbed her clean. I bent down and towel dried her legs in turn from her ankles.

"Thanks Terry."

I looked up at her, a bit surprised. This was her first interaction with me and judging by her face she seemed less distant than before, smiling, and for a moment recognising me. "I need to sleep now, Terry," she said.

I changed her and put her back to bed. Two hours later I went up with a cup of tea, pulled back the covers encouraging her to use the loo again and maybe get up and move around but all she wanted to do was sleep.

It didn't take me too long to realise that she had no control over her bodily functions and was incapable of doing anything herself. The moment I woke up I could smell the bed I was sharing was soiled and would have to get her up, strip her off and put her on the toilet while I washed her and the bedding again. It was like looking after a baby. Before she went to bed I wrapped her bottom area in a bath towel using it like a makeshift nappy at least containing any accidents in the night. I kept her in towels during the day as well and found I was washing them three or four times a day to cope with the demand.

I got through the first few weeks, settling back into home life as a full time carer. I noticed Ann's health start to deteriorate, particularly her state of mind. One minute she would boss me around like the old Ann and then suddenly change and I wouldn't get a word from her for hours. She seemed withdrawn and then she would repeat herself, asking the same question over and over again. I found out from her doctor that she had suffered from depression while I was away. It wasn't depression – it was much more than that.

2. Spot the Ball. 1993

"Terryy!"

I stood distracted for a moment, looking upwards at my conifers which were only supposed to grow to five foot. These rockets were double that.

I was at the bottom of the garden inspecting a section of fence fallen down in the night from heavy winds. I planted the trees when we first moved, wondering at the time if I'd planted them too far apart, because now these skyscrapers had taken over and joined together as one massive dense screen of green, blocking out the park at the back and the kids playing there.

It was roughly a hundred foot in distance from the front bedroom but I could still hear her. I ignored her at first, lifting, pushing the broken timber panel back into place but she got much louder and was screeching, singing my name so loud, staff at the post office on the main road would hear.

"TERRRRRRRRRRRRRRRYYYYYYYYYYY!" In the end I let the panelled fence fall in defeat.

I trudged to the back door, cursing and swearing, pressing the heel of each boot into the concrete edge of the step and pulled them off. I'd been in the garden most of the morning and it's where I tried to be.

We moved into our council house back in 1982, and both front and back gardens were just steep slopes of grass with bald patches worn out by the previous tenants and their kids.

I emptied three tonnes of soil from the front, dividing it into three levelled tiers. I visualised how I wanted the garden to look and took into account height, structure, colour and texture of what I planted and even trained and shaped the hedges to grow and hemmed in a variety of vividly coloured plants and a variety of different shades of lush greenery, bushes and shrubs. It was my work of art. People stopped and stared, and if I was around, they would tell me how nice my garden was, which made it all worthwhile.

To me it wasn't just a garden, it was another world I could escape to and I did as much as I could. In the summer I'd get up an hour earlier for work and potter around the garden, watering and weeding. I loved that time of the morning when the only thing you hear is next door's cat ferreting through the bushes, looking for the birds and the whirring engine sound of the milkman getting closer. Today wasn't one of those moments. It was late morning and her time to wake up.

"TERRY!" I washed my hands, picked up her tray and went upstairs.

This was the start of Ann's day. A mug of tea with two sweeteners and chocolate. KitKat was favourite at that moment. She'd stay loyal to one for a few months, get fed up and send me down the shop for something else. A Star Bar, Double Decker, Twix, Marathon (now Snickers), Aero, Topic and a Bounty.

She loved chocolate and her chubby five-foot figure showed it. Not just for breakfast either, she'd have two or three bars for lunch then sick them up in the toilet and pretend she never had them. Breakfast was always followed by smoking a couple of Superkings and doing *The Sun* crossword (with the help of a Collins dictionary she kept hidden under the bed). In fact, she couldn't do crosswords without one and always insisted on showing me when she finished. I found her secret hiding place and she got all defensive when I accused her of using it for crosswords.

I stood filling the doorway, with a tea towel over one arm. "Breakfast for the Queen," I announced and bowed. It didn't go down well; she just glared at me.

"Don't be so stupid, I thought you'd gone to work."

She sat regally, propped upright by pillows as I walked around the bed. Nose up, one arm behind my back, I strode around the bed, mocking her with my posh behaviour.

15

"Well ma lady, we seem to have a spot of bother. I've just arranged for the stable hands to saddle up your favourite Palomino but James wanted to bring the Rolls out around the front so I need to ask you; horse or—"

"Will you stop that? Why d'you have to be so stupid and why aren't you at work?"

Before I could answer, someone else was shouting my name.

"TERRY."

"I'm gonna change my name."

"What for?"

"Because every prat keeps calling it."

"Terry...don't swear," she said, completely missing my insult.

Ann hated swearing, even the word 'prat', not just from me either. We could be anywhere, like the time on a bus when two blokes in front of us started swearing and so she stood up and told them off. "Do you have to use that sort of language?" She didn't care, she was fearless.

I placed the tray on her lap and went to the window.

James Gardens is horseshoe-shaped with two junctions out onto the main road. Our elevated council house was at the U-bend part of the cul-de-sac overlooking the shortcut footpath to the shops.

"Don't open that!" Too late. I gripped, jerking the handle upwards cracking splintering, the paint off as I prised it open. We never used this window and had lacquered the metal frame with thick coats of white gloss when we moved in.

It was John. He was waving his paper at me. Seeing him reminded me of our newspaper. Where was it?

John knew everyone and everyone knew John. He was the eyes and ears of the estate and when the police turned up from time to time, John would be outside like a shot, asking questions like he was a policeman himself. If he didn't know he'd find out, then spread the word like the Messiah. He just made it his business to know everyone else's business and was always first to get his paper in the morning.

Shop staff would unbolt the door and find him waiting on the doorstep as their first customer, and today was no exception.

"Hey, your Mrs has won." His voice rushed into the room as I pushed the window out. "You've won!" he bellowed at me again.

"John, I can hear you now, you don't have to shout, mate."

"Who's that?" said Ann behind me.

I quickly turned back. "It's John."

"Won what?" I said, now leaning forward a bit to hear his answer.

"Spot the ball."

"John who?" said Ann.

"John, number nineteen John."

"Which one's nineteen again?" She said it more to herself this time and started counting door numbers on her fingers.

Irritated by the three-way conversation taking place, I ignored Ann and hung further out of the window to talk to John.

"Second prize she's won, it says here," now tapping his rolled up paper.

This made me laugh. "Shouldn't I know about this first?"

"It says here," said John. Now with something to prove he opens unravelling the pages quoting slowly. "This week's second prize winners of a Ford Fiesta or £7500 in cash are Mr J Dale, Carlisle and Mrs A Johnson, James Gardens, Plymouth." He looked up. "That's you. There's no other A Johnson round here. It's your Mrs."

Littlewoods always pinpointed the winner by advertising not only the surname but the city and the first line of the address.

"What's he saying?" said Ann, frowning with frustration trying to get back into the loop of chat.

"Apparently you've won Spot the Ball."

"What?"

"Terry."

"TERRY! Answer me…"

I hung back out the window again, laughing at the situation, but John's face remained serious.

17

"Yeh right." I wanted to believe him.

"If we've won Spot the Ball, shouldn't we know about it?"

"It's Bank Holiday today. No post."

"Ahh, that'll be it then." That's why Ann couldn't do her crossword. Bank Holiday... our paper boy's lie in today, bless him, no post and no *Sun* for Ann. He watched my reaction change on the doorstep when I saw Ann's name in print. "Back in a sec," I told him and disappeared with his paper leaping the stairs in twos to show Ann.

The next day she tore at the letter after seeing her name on the Liverpool post-marked envelope and held the cheque out, admiring it. "Seven thousand, five hundred pounds. Oh my giddy aunt. Well, I'll go to the foot of our stairs," she said.

It was more money than we'd ever seen. We've both been quite lucky over the years. She won the same competition in 1978, the second prize back then was £500 but it still paid for us to fly to Canada to see my mother and sister for three weeks. I also won £1300 in 1980 after doing a five-horse accumulator from a 10p stake.

Today it was a choice between a Ford Fiesta and the cash. Neither of us could drive so we took the cash.

"A holiday?" I said.

"We could do with a holiday." I could tell Ann had other ideas.

After banking the cheque we left town with a pile of brochures and spent the evening at our pine table and bench trying to sell her my idea. We could never afford holidays abroad so to suddenly have all this choice was a bit overwhelming. I got an old Atlas out of the cupboard, scanning the pages across Europe and followed my finger down into Africa. I had always had a thing about Africa. I left school without any qualifications except geography. Geography was my thing, it was then and it still is now. I amazed the teacher with a mark of ninety-eight per cent in the exam, which from the school drop out, surprised them. I'd always had a genuine curiosity and a thirst for knowledge about different countries, cultures and climates around the world. I also remember doing a school project all about Africa which I was extremely proud of.

I liked learning about exotic countries around the equator with their extreme environments, so different to ours, and the wild animals who are free to roam. I loved watching David Attenborough's *Assignment in Africa*. My favourite animal is the cheetah. It mesmerises me with its power and grace as it sprints at speed to chase and overpower its prey.

My finger stopped at Kenya on the map. I looked at Ann. "That's the place." Christmas in Africa it was then. I could tell by her reaction that she wasn't totally sold on the idea until I mentioned her mum and dad.

Ann rang her parents that night and surprised them with a free holiday to Kenya. They were in their seventies and had never been on a plane before, so we were all excited and couldn't wait for Christmas.

"The Shelly Beach Hotel. The hotel is south of Mombasa, commands a view over the warm clear waters of the Indian Ocean and a sweeping stretch of white sugary sand of Diani Beach, with palm trees that gently bow in the tropical sea breeze." That'll do.

The ten-hour flight offered a free bar which I took full advantage of with a steady supply of my favourite drink – Bacardi and Coke.

Ann was never a big drinker; more than one or two gave her headaches so instead she kept the air stewardess busy asking for chocolate they didn't stock and in the end settling for anything they did have washed down with Diet Coke, heading straight for the loo after.

The hotel didn't have a lift so I booked a ground floor room and made sure the complex didn't have too many steps for the old man. The only thing I didn't expect was small grit-like stones laid unevenly around the pool, which was a problem. He wobbled on his stick as we took each arm and moved slowly around the pool to find a suitable spot. We made sure they were both shaded, keeping

19

their milky white skin from the sun. I tipped one of the staff who made a fuss of us every time we came out and would always go to the trouble of moving a thatched roof parasol which he positioned over them.

"Come on, father, let's go." I stood up with my hands on my hips. "Come on, up you get." He lifted his floppy hat-wearing head and looked at me as if I was insane.

"What?"

"Swimming. Come on, let's go."

"No way." Folding, locking his arms together with a face like thunder.

I did manage to lure him away but that was for sneaky drinks. He liked a drink and I got the feeling he didn't get much chance at home.

It wasn't 'all inclusive' back then so I made sure I bought a large bottle of Bacardi from duty free and kept it in my case. Every morning, a couple of hours after breakfast, I'd give him the signal and off we went back to the room, and by midday, I'd have the old boy singing, feeling the full effect of the booze with his Mrs giving us both a stern look over her glasses. I liked him like this. A few drinks and the child came out, his expression softened and when he creased a smile, his eyes twinkled with mischief.

The last time he swam was when he was a kid, and now sixty years on I finally got him in the pool. Ann's mum sat under the parasol, looking up over her book at us as we splashed each other like kids. She was a bit of a stick in the mud most of the time but I managed to loosen father up with a few sneaky drinks.

One afternoon, a couple of beach boys managed to attract his attention as he got out of the pool. They were sitting on the perimeter wall. I was amazed that he actually went over to them (that'll be the Bacardi again).

These boys made their living from selling tourists souvenirs and they could only pester you outside the hotel. We couldn't hear them but we watched the body language of these two dark lean figures, loaded with merchandise, interacting with this pasty white old man smeared white with sun cream in his big cargo shorts and floppy hat. They each had their arms coated in shiny necklaces and half a dozen pairs of sunglasses on their head. I was on the verge of rescuing him but then he wobbled back to us, shaking his head.

"God Almighty!" he shouted at us over the pool, marching back to us. "God Almighty, do you know what they just said to me? They said, 'Eh mister, when you die will you give us your false teeth'?"

We all cracked up at the shock and seriousness of his face. Pointing back, he said, "He wants my false teeth." He kept repeating it, which made us laugh even more.

"Don't worry, dad," I said. "I'll send them when you've gone."

The holiday really seemed to rejuvenate the old boy. I've never seen him laugh so much, and after a few wobbly days, he left his stick in the room and never used it again, even his posture changed and for two weeks he stopped being an old man.

That afternoon I got talking to reception and learnt a few more things about the beach boys. From time to time, the local papers featured stories about them and public debate would usually form the opinion they were a bloody nuisance.

On the south coast the hotels are more expensive and the beach boys are under stricter control. Three or four would only be allowed to patrol the tide edge and wait for an invite, they weren't allowed to approach you but a lot of time they did. Hotels didn't want them around hassling, upsetting their guests.

What to do about them was a general concern. The beach boys were street vendors who sold anything to make a living. Most came from the city selling ornaments, jewellery, hats, sunglasses which they loaded up from shops early in the morning and got the ferry across to the hotels and beaches along the south coast. That was one reason I didn't like the beach. First timers to Kenya make the mistake once of going on the beach and then they try their best to avoid it for the rest of the holiday. Beach boys take it in turns, following you about, and simply won't take no for an answer.

The heat and the drink seemed to make mum and especially dad sleepy, so by the afternoon they were ready for a snooze. We'd get back to our rooms at about four in the afternoon so they could rest and then get ready for dinner. I enjoyed the transformation of a warm shower, shirt and trousers after an oily, sweaty day in the sun.

Like most afternoons I left them all to it. Ann went into their room to wake them and help her dad get dressed. His joints were badly disfigured with arthritis and had trouble dressing himself, so to give mum a break, she spent the holiday helping him. Ready and not needed, I went down to the bar for a sneaky B and C. It was early and not many guests were around so I just sat at the bar. I wasn't there long when I felt the presence of someone near me.

"Ok old man, you buy me omelette and chips, ok?" said the African voice. I could tell she was talking to me without even looking at her. The barman opposite stood polishing a glass and looked straight at me, waiting for my reaction.

"Yep, no problem," and I repeated the order to the barman, still not fully acknowledging her, but when I did, I saw a woman no more than twenty-one with a complexion so smooth she didn't look real. She had a real cheeky glint in her big brown eyes. I knew straight away she was going to be fun. The barman shook his head disapprovingly and she snapped back, "I'm a guest, room 134, and before you ask, my boyfriend has the key." The barman left us to it. "He's going to reception to check," she said.

The food arrived and I watched her shovel it down. "Eh slow down, you'll get indigestion." As I said this so she seemed to eat faster, and kept looking at the door. "You're not really staying here, are you?"

She nodded, trying to clear a mouthful of food. "I am, I'm with you." She was now grinning and winking.

"My wife takes up too much room in the bed for you as well."

She cackled and started to choke. Her eyes watered so I slid my beer across the bar and she took a gulp, laughing and trying to breathe all at the same time.

"You," she said, pointing her knife at me, "are funny, old man."

Of course, compared to her I was old, by about forty years. I didn't take offence, she was so charming, a straight talker and said things how they were. No bullshit and I liked that. In fact I never asked her real name either and made hers up on the spot – Madam, to me she was a Madam.

I told her she spoke really good English. "You have to if you want to survive in Mombasa. For us it's all about the mzungu." She could tell this was the first time I'd heard this word. She pointed at me. "You mzungu, white man." Most white people speak English so we have to learn it. I know German and French but mainly English. Local girls are not allowed into hotels unless they are with a paying guest so we have to make friends with a mzungu. Sometimes I stay here but it's been quiet. It's not been a good few weeks, I've not eaten for a while."

"No shit," I said, which made her laugh again.

She pushed the empty plate away, thanking me just as the barman returned.

"Thank you old man, thank you. Enjoy your holiday and a big kiss for your wife." She kissed her palm and threw it back at me and I watched her curves sashay towards the door.

I finished my drink and moved into lounge to wait for the others to come down. I sat there thinking about this young girl. I admired her cheeky, direct style. I could tell she survived by instinct and I liked that.

I went down to the bar the next day about the same time hoping to see her again but it was three days later when I did. I had the paper open on the bar when she crept up beside me. "Boo!" I jumped, crunching the pages together in shock and she laughed.

"Not you again. Don't tell me," I said, holding my hand up. "You want omelette and chips again?"

"No."

"I've come to buy you a drink."

"Aah I see, you buy me the drink and I've got to get the omelette and chips again. Very clever."

"No." She started fishing around in her bag. "I'm staying here with a client and I want to buy you a drink."

She did and as quick as my drink was served she was gone again.

The holiday seemed to change us all in some ways. The old boy swam nearly every day and told me he felt alive again, even the mother-in-law cracked a few more smiles than normal. Ann spent the whole holiday fussing around after them both which made her happy and left me alone to wander. I had this little routine going. I use to get up about six every morning and watch the hotel come alive. I'd get a coffee and sit near reception and watch the staff interact with each other. I could see the way they spoke and behaved; they were more relaxed without guests around. The same girls every morning mopped the foyer floor, smiled hello and the receptionist on seeing me handed me my newspaper, a week old didn't matter, never really read it anyway. It was my cover. I'd sit out the way and just watch.

A bit later I'd move and perch on a stool at the same bar where I'd met Madam and wait for the duty manager, who on arrival, went straight behind the bar. Keeping one eye on the paper and the other on him I watched him count everything in the bar and I mean everything; bottles, glasses, ashtrays even the straws were emptied, counted individually and put back in the box. He finished his stock take by measuring and marking the spirit bottles and made a note of everything.

It was clear to see from his efforts that everything behind that bar had a value which he was responsible for – he needed to be conscientious and couldn't afford mistakes.

Just after he went, another person arrived to stock the bar. His name was George and was from a village on the outskirts. He cycled in, worked fourteen hours and cycled home again. He did this six times a week for £30 a month. We would chat until the manager showed up again and I could see this made him nervous so I'd stop talking and pick up my paper again. One morning he rushed into the bar and the manager called him into the back room. I couldn't understand a word, but their actions were the universal language of a bollocking. He grabbed his bag and I saw him with his bike through the window. I got up and followed him, shouting his name. He turned and circled around back to me. It turned out he was a few minutes late so they sent him home and that meant no money for him or his family. That was harsh but a good way for the hotel to save money when it wasn't busy. The next morning he came in making sure he was early this time. I called him over and handed him a thousand bob.

"What's that for?"

"Don't be late again."

"You are crazy man, thank you. Thank you very much."

To me, Kenya was much more than a holiday. It was the start of a love affair but I knew I would soon be back in the cold and miserable darkness of January in England.

3. Shopping & Bulimia

I started working on a new site for a company who were building a hundred new homes over the next three years so it meant plenty of work for me. I worked for a subcontractor and we had to landscape the gardens which involved laying lawns or paving outside areas. As each wave of properties were finished we were sent in to sort the garden and green areas out before the new owners moved in, so we were up against it as far as time was concerned. I didn't drive so had to rely on workmates to pick me up.

Owning a car had never interested me. I had a Triumph 650 when I was twenty, but never bothered taking driving lessons in a car. I worked on farms back then and could easily handle a tractor or a digger. At times I wished I'd passed my test because I had to put up with waiting around for lifts, relying on them to turn up on time and to drive properly with me in the car. I normally worked six ten-hour days with Sunday off; it was hard graft which didn't faze me. I was, in many people's view, a grafter and was never short of work. The money never matched my efforts though. I always did the donkey work and made other people money. I should have taken more risks back then and turned that around so I was the one making the money but I just settled for being 'Terry the Grafter'.

Work and my garden occupied my life but I couldn't stop thinking about Kenya. I kept these thoughts alive by reading.

Apart from the racing pages of newspapers I'd never been into reading books. Never had the patience or attention span, but that soon changed. I started reading, absorbing facts, details about the history, the culture and the language. I was obsessed. I even bought an audio language course from W.H. Smith, and by sheer fluke came across an old Swahili dictionary at a car boot sale. I spent hours writing, revising and cross-referencing different words and their meaning. Most of what I did at work involved digging holes so I went into autopilot mode and my mind drifted to Kenya. Africa had seduced me and I needed to see her again.

Ann was now well and truly into her bulimic phase. I use the word 'phase' because that's what it was with her, a phase. The occasional session had now become a daily thing. She went through all sorts of faddy diets, a shake for breakfast, shake for lunch type thing, which worked for a while until she lost interest.

She missed her chocolate too much. So she was now eating four/five bars a day followed by the fingers down the throat routine. She tried to be discreet about it all but no matter how much bleach she squirted down the loo I could still smell vomit. Deep down she knew I knew but I couldn't help her. It was impossible to help her, and if I confronted her about it she would do her usual and deny it, then if I pushed it she'd get angry. In the end, she got fed up of raking her throat but carried on eating the chocolate and put all the weight back on.

I sat down one night and worked out the bills. I hadn't done this for a while and needed to see how much I could save to get us back to Africa. I worked out we still had prize money left over so it wouldn't be that difficult to save the rest – that was until Ann got her hands on the money.

I finished a job early one Friday afternoon and got a lift back to an empty house, which was strange – she never went out. A few hours later while watching tv, I heard the humming of a diesel engine outside and shot to the door. I stood in the doorway looking down as Ann pulled bag after bag out of the taxi.

"Come and help me, Terry." I sloped down the steps in no rush, dreading the worst. Debenhams, House of Fraser, Argos, etc. She'd been busy. Our front room was like the *Generation Game*. A candy floss maker, sandwich maker, I picked up the boxed Kenwood chef mixer. "But you don't even fucking bake cakes."

"Don't swear and don't start. I've decided I'm going to start cooking, be more like my mother." She would always involve her mother in the conversation. Mother was like royalty she put her on a pedestal like she was the Queen and was desperate to be just like her. I knew most of the things she bought that day would stay boxed and would never be used. I later found out this wasn't the first taxi shopping trip since winning Spot the Ball. She used our neighbour's house to hide it from me. Then right in front of me she tipped the driver with a fiver – like we had money to burn.

I moved through the pile of bags, looking at what else she bought. "This is all crap, all fucking crap. I can't believe you've wasted the money on this shit." Ann had wasted just over three grand and I hated her for it.

"I won the money so it's up to me how we spend it," was her response. My dream of a return to Africa was like the money – fading fast. Seven and a half thousand quid is more money than I've ever had or probably will ever see in my lifetime and to spend nearly half of it in this way made me angry.

Normally she didn't need money, which made wasting it on this lot even more insulting. If she couldn't buy it, she'd nick it. She had an amazing talent for shoplifting. She'd go into town with a couple of quid in her pocket for the taxi home and return hours later with her tartan shopping trolley stuffed with goodies. I knew she had a problem but there was no way of helping her. If I confronted her with questions she'd lie. She was devious and a quick thinker and could act out of most situations, especially when she got caught.

She'd break down in the street crying, convincing the store detective with a sob story, shocked at her own behaviour which was totally out of character – and it worked. She could switch her expression, widen her eyes, adding a much softer tone of voice than her normal throaty smoker's one and she was totally believable. After fifteen years she had become my specialist subject, but even so, if I confronted her and pushed the issue, she got aggressive. A foot in height separates us but that didn't make a difference, as I had learnt over the years. Ann feared nothing and no-one; I still have the scars from her sovereign rings to prove it.

When we first moved into our council house, a lot of kids used to hang around outside on the street sometimes playing football or kerby, and when the ball landed in our garden they never knocked on the door to ask, they just helped themselves. One evening while watching tv, Ann reacted to noise just outside the window and leaping up, opening the door shouting, "Oi! What d'you think you're doing?"

I followed her to the door and a lad was stood in the middle of our garden holding the ball and flowers he'd just picked. His mates were looking up from the road cheering, goading him on. Ann lurched forward grabbed this kid's arm and pulled him to the steps.

"Hey, fucking leave him alone," the biggest lad spoke up.

Ann glared at him, let go of the kid and flew down the steps quicker than I've ever seen her move. Now fearing the worst, I followed behind her, trying to calm her down. She strode up to the kid, who was the size of a minibus and had no choice but to look up at him.

"What did you just say?"

"I said, fucking leave him alone."

It wasn't a punch, more of a palm shove to his chin which made him step backwards. That shook him up. His face flushed red, embarrassed in front of his mates. He wasn't expecting that from this five foot nothing permed warrior and could see by her mad stare she wasn't going to back down. She stepped closer to him with both fists clenched, waiting for his reaction. His mates were telling him to leave it, which he wisely did. Ann did what she always did and stood her ground.

After her spending spree I did think about encouraging her back to work. We could save which would take the burden off me a bit, but I knew that would be a mistake. In twenty years together she had only had two other jobs. It was safer for everyone concerned if she kept away from money and anything of any value.

A local supermarket took her on a trial basis and the first week they trained her on the tills and she did really well. Customers loved her confidence and loud bubbly personality, especially the oldies and she always seemed to have more pensioners in her queue than anyone else. In fact, regulars would ignore smaller queues at other checkouts just so they could have a little natter with Annie, as they called her, and if that meant waiting longer, then they did. The boss was chuffed with her high level of customer service, took her on full time with plenty of overtime – everything was going well until the results of the quarterly stock-take showed a big deficit. Head office got involved and sent down an auditor to troubleshoot and find out where the store was leaking money. The loss was pinpointed to one area – the fresh meat counter. Staff were watched, searched leaving work and random checks at the tills were made. Even customer receipts were checked against the shopping they had and Ann was finally caught. She had been more or less giving away joints of meat to the pensioners coming through her till. She did this Robin Hood thing of marking down a rib of beef down to say thirty-six pence or even pushing it through free of charge. She was taking from a super rich company and dishing it out to the hard-up oldies. It was stealing with a conscience and that's why she was so popular.

When they caught her, she asked the manager how on earth did he expect these poor pensioners to be able to afford their Sunday lunch? That was her reasoning and the fact she wasn't caught nicking it for herself, they decided not to involve the police, they just got rid of her.

The same thing happened at the Wimpy Bar which opened in our town back in the late seventies and caused a bit of fuss. Ann spent a lot of time there eating Brown Derbys and Coke floats. She openly flirted with the owner, a Greek guy who took a shine to her. He owned the franchise and always seemed to be short staffed.

"The problem is Andreas, you take on kids who like to party and you pay them peanuts; that's why they never turn up for work. You need someone special working here, someone a bit more mature, someone reliable and you need to pay them well." She badgered him every time she went in and it wasn't long before she talked herself into a job.

The customers loved her and the boss was more than happy with how things were going and could see with Ann's ability he could relax a bit more. He loved the horses and began spending more time down the bookies and trusted Ann to run the place, ordering stock, organising and recruiting staff. She was given keys to the restaurant and had full access to the safe. She became his unofficial manageress, unofficial because he never paid her extra and had no intention of doing so.

It didn't take long for things to go wrong. She gave most of what she cooked away to family and friends and the pensioners found out where she worked and that was the end of that.

The job she had when we first met was at the hospital. She told me she was a qualified nurse. She had always had an ambition to be a nurse even at school but and it wasn't until I had an accident at work that I found out the truth. I needed stitches in my hand and my boss at the time drove me to the same hospital that Ann worked at. Ann had finished her shift by then and was at home and I got chatting to the nurse stitching my hand.

I remembered the colour of Ann's uniform so I asked this nurse the difference between her blue one and Ann's brown one. Blue was for a qualified registered nurse and brown was for an auxiliary nurse. She wasn't even a qualified nurse. Making tea, cleaning, making up the beds and bed baths; that was her job. Ann was just the nurse's assistant, not qualified to treat patients but that didn't stop her telling everybody she was. I can't remember why she left but she came home one day and said she'd had enough. That didn't stop her playing nurse at home though. Over the years I learnt to keep boils, spots, cuts and splinters to myself because out came her surgical scissors, cotton wool and TCP, leaving me in more pain and discomfort than before. "Come on, I used to be a nurse, don't be silly, let me look at it." Those words made me run.

I didn't need the hassle and worry of Ann going back to work, so I knew I had to do something about it myself. I was so focused on getting back to Kenya that I took on more work, cutting hedges for my neighbours. They could see how good I was at cutting mine and I had quite a few customers, which made it a nice little sideline. After a day's graft on the sites and some food, I was out trimming hedges until it was too dark to carry on. This time I made sure I kept this money away from Ann and had an arrangement with the travel agent where I could go in and pay the holiday off in chunks so she couldn't spend it.

4. Robbed in Africa

We decided to go back to the same hotel but this time we went with Ted and Rita. I worked with Ted who was so fed up with me constantly talking about Kenya that he and his Mrs decided to come with us.

The staff remembered me from the year before and I knew it was going to be fun. The hotel was managed by Asians who were, as I found out, very strict with their staff; everything was organised military style. Every couple of days at roughly the same time in the afternoon the big boss did his tour of duty but I got the feeling it was more to do with his own self-importance, shiny suit and clipboard than checking hotel standards. In full view of the holidaymakers he paraded around the pool with his second in command in tow; tapping, kicking, squinting and scribbling things down as he went. All the staff stood around to attention as their areas were inspected and they all took it very seriously.

One afternoon, I told George the barman to expect some fun at inspection. He'd got to know me quite well now so was dreading the outcome. "Oh God, what are you going to do now, you crazy man?"

I stood just inside the bar and waited for the boss man to pass me and start his outside inspection, then I followed him, keeping a short distance behind him but in full view of the staff who were now in position. When he moved I moved, copying his actions, looking up when he did, looking down and even scribbled on my pretend clipboard. When he did turn around, I made sure I was quicker, pretending to look down at the pool, waiting and sensing that he wasn't looking, I carried on following him around the pool. I could tell the guests were now used to this ceremony and more or less ignored him and me in my trunks behind mimicking him

33

and still holding my Bacardi and Coke, but the staff didn't and did their best to hide their smiles in front of their strict boss. The Towel Lady who spotted me from the start stood by the towel hut waiting. As he got nearer she did her best to contain herself while I did my Mr Bean impression behind him. The second he passed her she started shaking and stifling the noise with her hand across her mouth. Later that evening, all the staff took turns cursing me but it did brighten up their day so it was all good.

About half way through the holiday we decided to venture out of the hotel and discover Mombasa for the first time. The reps in the welcome meeting warned us about the dangers and crime in the city but that didn't put us off.

We had forty quid to put into Barclays and we found out they had a branch in the city so we booked a taxi there and back. I took on board the reps' advice but thought as long as we keep to the main streets then we would be fine and I took the whole carrying money thing very seriously. I put the money into a wallet and put it into the side pocket of a hessian style shopping bag, and as we left our room I hooped the handles together looping it up one arm and over my shoulder, gripping the bag tight into my armpit. No swine was going to get my money. When we got to Barclays the first thing I noticed was the guard sat slouched near the door, not reacting to the chaos unfolding. There was no organised queuing system; people were pushing and shoving, trying their best to get served first. First thing we did was sit down and wait but the bank seemed to get busier so in the end we joined in jostling for position and finally it was our turn. I straightened my arm, sliding the handles down over my wrist opening, delving into the side pocket for my wallet and it wasn't there. Ann could see my expression change as I rooted through the bag.

"What's the matter?" I didn't answer.

"You've lost it, haven't you?"

I kept my hand moving and felt the holes, one in the bottom and another in the side pocket compartment. "I've been robbed," I said, staring at her.

I stood in disbelief opening the bag as wide as I could so she could see for herself. I smiled as she looked back after checking the bag. "Well it's not funny is it? Gimme that," she said, snatching the bag from me. The guard at the door was gone. Ann took a few seconds to react and then rattled her knuckles on the glass to get the cashier's attention.

"Right, where's the boss? Where's your manager? Get him out here now. My husband has been robbed here in your bank. The guard is in on it too, look," she said, pointing at the empty chair by the door. "He's disappeared as well, that says it all."

A man appeared from behind glass marked 'Private'. He was short and porky in size and wore a belt so tight it squeezed his fat into a rubber ring. He reached up for the top bolt, showing us his underarm sweat patches on his white shirt. Looking at us over his glasses which balanced over the end of his nose, he rattled the keys to unlock the swing door underneath the counter, which he lifted up. As he did so, Ann rushed through the gap, pushing past and into the back office where she let rip, not giving him a chance to answer.

"You must be in on it as well. How can you let this happen in your bank? And where is your guard? Fat lot of good he is or is he on a cut too?" She sat with her arms folded and I stood behind her while the manager used the phone. Ann got up and went behind the counter. "Come on, get up," she barked at the cashier, taking her seat and sat there clutching her bag staring back through the glass as more customers came in to see what all the fuss was about.

"Take your money away," she ranted at them. "Don't use Barclays. Barclays bank is a nightmare. How can they let this happen? This place is a mess, just like a cattle market. When I get home I'm going to put in a big complaint."

She stood and pointed at the staff stood to one end. "I want you all to sort this bloody mess out." The sit-in demonstration at the bank was typical Ann.

While the manager was on the phone, the other cashier started to explain things to me. She took hold of my bag, folding it back, inspecting the holes. "Razors. They used a razor to slice your bag."

Razors were a very useful tool for the criminals in Kenya. Police stop and search and check the hiding place for a razor – under the tongue. Police can normally get a good idea about a suspect's past by the condition of their mouth which is sliced and scarred from keeping razors in it. Razors were the tools of their trade, and under the tongue was the best place to hide them but the first place police checked.

Not sure if this ever happened again but when I went back to the bank a few years later it seemed more organised with one main queue and closed circuit tv cameras had been fitted.

Police turned up and didn't seem interested, by which time Ann had simmered down a bit and reminded the bank manager about the formal complaint she was pursuing before we left.

Ann never really got over the robbery; it spoilt her holiday. She was really angry about the whole situation. I guess she wasn't used to being the victim.

I was more in awe of the way I was robbed. Whoever stood behind me had the guile and the skill of a surgeon to slice open the bag, reach in, slice the other inside pocket and take my wallet without me feeling a thing. Bloody incredible. If they are that good and prepared to go that far then fair play. They deserve my money.

We got back to the hotel and told Ted and Rita what had happened at the bank and, like us, they couldn't believe it. Ann's enthusiasm for the rest of the holiday changed. It wasn't just the robbery. She found the weather too hot and wasn't a big drinker as one or two drinks gave her headaches, so I would go on a walkabout, making friends, leaving her plugged into a Walkman under a parasol.

The determination to rob me that day was the first of many insights into Kenyans who are prepared to do what's necessary to survive.

Home and the normality of work was again a reality. Ann was up to her tricks again. She shouted at me to come in from the garden and told me she had problems with her sight. Her head tilted back, I used two fingers to stretch both eyes wide open to see if I could see anything which was causing her eyes to be so inflamed and when I told her I couldn't see anything and that maybe it was a bit of grit that was irritating her, she said, "Terry, it's more than that, everything is blurred." I settled her down with wet cotton pads on each eye and told her to relax.

About an hour later she screamed my name. I rushed upstairs and she was holding the pads, looking around the room.

"I'm going blind," she said. The thing was, I never trusted anything she said, and the truth was, I couldn't be sure and thought it was best to get her checked out.

So we got a taxi to the eye hospital where the doctor examined her, gave her some drops and told her, once the irritation went, her vision should be back to normal. A lot of the blurred vision had been caused by her rubbing them.

As we left, she grabbed hold of my arm and started stumbling into people and empty chairs in the waiting room. We got outside the main entrance and a nurse who had seen us earlier appeared with a white stick and gave it to Ann. Over the next two weeks that white stick became the bane of my life. She wasn't blind enough to dig out a small brass bell from one of the drawers and use it everytime she needed me. I didn't see my garden for a week because I wouldn't hear that fucking bell in the garden.

I sat in the dining room, smoking and thinking about where I would like to be while she sat in the living room surrounded by chocolate wrappers and Coke, listening to the *Carpenters* or Bette Davis movies. She even wore her sunglasses around the house because she said the light hurt her eyes. One time I caught her out though, she thought I was outside but I peered into the room and she sat there with her sunglasses on her forehead, flicking through the *TV Times*. I paced slowly, quietly back to the door, opening then closing it, and walked into the front room to find Ann laid back with her sunglasses on.

"Is that you, Terry?"

"Who else would it fucking be?"

"Don't swear, you know it upsets me."

I could have made a big thing about it but I knew it would make no difference. I just carried on playing her game. Ann was Ann, and nothing, not even the truth, could change that, so for an easy life I went along with everything as usual.

5. My New Life

When I did get back out into the garden, I borrowed her Walkman and spent hours weeding, pruning, listening to the Swahili words being played into my ears. I amused the kids walking up to the park who could hear me blurt out this weird sounding language, and when I wasn't listening to it, I used to practise writing it from my dictionary. It was during Ann's 'blindness' episode that helped me make a life-changing decision. I was fifty-six years old and the thought of retiring, not working and putting up with all the shit from Ann depressed me. If I didn't plan something now I never would.

I could have kept it simple, stayed local but away from Ann. A one-bed garden flat somewhere where I could retire in peace. But that wasn't enough and I wanted more. I wanted a new life. I wanted adventure and excitement. I was tired of scraping by, busting my bollocks for other people, coming home and having to hide in my garden for a peaceful life. I wanted to live again. I wanted to experience new things, meet new people and get as far away from here as I could and I knew just the place.

The Swahili I knew would improve if I was there all the time and maybe I could get a job helping out with safaris. I planned to save three months' wages and then I would be off. I couldn't sleep and my head buzzed with ideas. I felt like a teenager; excited, not sure how things would pan out but full of optimism. I had a good feeling about this and always went with my instincts. I had to do it.

It took me two years to plan and save but I had to escape. The 16th March 1997 as far as Ann was concerned, was just another day at work for me. I put money and a note in an envelope on her breakfast tray and left it on the chest of drawers while she slept.

Ann,

All the bills are up to date and this is food money for the next few months.

I will try and send you more as and when I can to help you out.

I'm not coming back.

Look after yourself.

Terry

The taxi pulled away and my life was about to change. I felt no sadness, regret or guilt, just a tingle in my stomach which told me I was a little bit nervous but I'd put up with Ann's shit for years and I felt like I was rebelling against a strict parent.

I booked a two-week stay back at my favourite hotel and the plan was to find somewhere cheaper and find work as soon as I could after that. The staff, especially George, recognised me. "Hey, crazy man is back, but where is your wife?"

I stood at his bar sipping the first B+C of my new life and told him.

"I don't have a wife. No wife anymore." Winking at his smiling face I walked away.

"Crazy man is back," I said, raising my glass in the air as I walked away. I made my way out of the seating area at the back of the hotel and onto the beach where two enthusiastic beach boys bounded up to me, arms dripping with souvenirs, and introduced themselves.

"Hey mister, my name is Del Boy, you know Fools and Horses?" turning to his mate who was no more than five foot tall, standing by his side. "This is Rodney, he's a plonker," he said, which sounded weird in his strong Kenyan accent. His mate kept quiet the whole time.

"It's *Only Fools and Horses*," I said, correcting him.

"Yes, yes, that's right."

"I have lovely jubbly things for you to buy." He gave the nod to Rodney.

"No, it's ok, I'm not interested."

It made no difference, his mate unfastened the bag on his hip and handed Del Boy a board of shiny rings and started going through each one.

"Look, this one for your wife, this one for your girlfriend," he said, winking at me. I kept saying no and I started to move away but he followed me, pushing his board into my face. His voice got louder and louder, drowning out my voice and then I told them to be quiet. "KUACHA KUZUMGUMZA!"

"Ah, you speak Swahili."

"Yes, I do. Now listen. I don't want to buy anything, ok? Nothing. But I do need your help and if you help me I will pay, ok?" I had their attention now and they both nodded back in silence. "I need to stay somewhere local for a few weeks. It's got to be nice and safe, understand? And it's got to be cheap. Meet me here two weeks from today at this time at this spot." I looked up as I spoke, taking in my surroundings.

"Yes sir, no problem."

"Don't forget, nice and cheap but no shit, ok?"

The following two weeks I hardly spent any time at the hotel and used taxis to get to know the other hotels along the coast. Two of the days I used to visit Mombasa. The only time I had been to Mombasa was back when I was robbed in Barclays and we didn't hang around to sight-see that day, so it was time to visit the place properly. I got reception to book a taxi and I explained to the driver I wanted to see the touristy stuff first then I wanted to see and learn new things. I wanted him to take me to see the real side of Kenya.

I didn't realise until I got there that the city of Mombasa is an island and it's only obvious at high tide. If you want to go north you have to go over Nyali Bridge and the only way you get to the south coast is on the Likoni Ferry. It crosses the Kilindini Harbour to the Kenyan mainland town of Likoni. Two double-ended ferries go back and forth packed, and I mean packed, with people and cargo. Vehicles pay a small charge, foot passengers go free. The crossing is only about five hundred metres but when these dilapidated vessels break down it can leave passengers stranded half way over for hours at a time. It's a real culture shock to see so many people, rusty old bikes and wooden carts on this floating rust bucket. Most of them go to the south coast for work or, like the beach boys, when they've got something to sell to the tourists. Blokes with carts use the ferry to take eight or nine large plastic containers full of water over from the mainland. The supply and distribution of water in Kenya can be a problem, especially in villages, so these lads used to earn money providing a service for those able to pay around thirty to fifty pence for a day's supply of water. I used to see them early in the morning getting off the ferry pushing, heaving half a tonne of water up a hundred metres of steep incline and then spend the rest of the day touring the areas, selling it. Those who could afford the water constantly made the choice between washing in it or drinking it, many recycled it for both.

When the ferry empties out at Likoni, a swarm of people move en masse up the steep slipway towards the hill past the garage and down to Diani Beach. For Shelly Beach you take a left turn at the garage and the narrow road, after about half a mile, comes to an end. The trees that line either side of the road get thicker for the monkeys that swing and jump between them, and at any point you can cut down to a quiet secluded beach where locals would wash and bathe, hidden away to carry on with the chores of their own lives, just up the road from the holidaymakers whose experience of Kenya would be a Safari or lounging by the pool eating and drinking in luxury, or being pestered by the beach boys.

Tourists were always advised to get a taxi to get about so they generally wouldn't get to see this side of Kenyan life, but I did - It was my desire to get to know the real Kenya.

6. The Landlord

Bob the taxi driver took me around for the next two days, stopping at places so he could explain things and answer my questions, and I always had a question for him. He told me his Kenyan name was too long so he called himself Bob. I found out a lot of Kenyans did this – it made it easier for the tourists to remember their names. He'd been a taxi driver for the last eleven years and lived in Likoni with his wife and three children. At the end of the second day I asked him to show me where he lives and where he goes for a beer.

He took me to a bar and I met some of his family and friends and we sat around talking. It was here I met the Landlord, or should I say the cowboy. He wore a white oversized Stetson, which looked like a plate of blancmange on his head. He was an African JR Ewing, just without the oil. He owned a compound of eight or nine houses which he rented out for about a thousand bob a month.

He walked over and interrupted us mid-flow in the conversation and asked me if I wanted to join his table, pointing over to it and the three girls sat there. I insisted we all went over and made one big group. The Landlord drank very quickly and started re-ordering but I told him I was on medication and one was my limit. I quickly decided at that moment that I needed to stay sober and did that a lot during my time over there. I was the only white man in their backyard and getting drunk could have made me a target for someone. It didn't stop him though, the man could definitely put them away. The girls didn't say much, but every time the Landlord left the table they talked quietly with me. I got talking with Sharon; she was twenty and worked in Mombasa as a hairdresser and came from a tribe in the north; she was much darker than the other two girls.

On the way back from the loo the Landlord collared me at the bar and told me Sharon was single and had taken a shine to me.

The girls were shy but every time the Landlord was around they seemed on edge. I took the chance of talking to them outside and they seemed to come alive smiling, and when the Landlord appeared, now the worse for wear, he gestured to them and they reacted instantly. I wondered what sort of hold he had over them but when I talked to others about him they just said he was friends with their parents and was quite protective over them. The only thing they did say was that he was a bit of an asshole when he got drunk, but apart from that he looked after their family.

Sharon was the only one that really spoke to me that day, so I thought her interest was genuine and I asked her out to dinner, and she said yes.

We went into Mombasa and she showed me where she worked. She loved talking. Her English was very good and she seemed well-educated. I stayed with her family for a few days. The house was made with breeze blocks a tin sheet roof and was divided into two rooms – one was the living/cooking area and a sheet of polythene hung as a door, separating the back room where she slept with her mother and sister.

We met up a few times and our relationship went from friends to lovers in a short space of time.

I went back to the hotel and finished the last few days by the pool, topping up the tan, sipping Bacardi and Coke through a straw, and when it got too hot, I dipped in the pool for a swim and it was here that my friend surprised me.

I swam half the pool underwater, bobbing up at the edge and hauled myself up at one end, propping myself up with my elbows, scraping water out of my eyes, keeping them closed and relaxing in the moment.

"Hello old man." I jumped back and spluttered, trying not to swallow water as I quickly closed my mouth again and went under.

As I resurfaced, bobbing up, she stood over me, cackling loudly.

It was Madam. She'd seen me in the pool and waited for her chance to lie down at the edge nose to nose with me and stayed there till I opened my eyes. She found my reaction hysterical, and she got up and waved. "I see you in the bar later."

It turned out she was staying with a German guy and would sneak down to the bar and meet me for a drink whenever she got the chance. We never arranged times but I made sure I was always in the same place at the same time to give us the chance of meeting up. Over the next few days I got to know more about her. She lived in one of the smaller villages on the outskirts of the city. I could tell by her sense of humour and beaming smile she was a survivor and she had that mischievous glint in her eyes, which I loved.

Every time we met she'd say the same thing. "Teach me English."

"No way, you don't need it, your English is fantastic."

"Teach me English phrase."

"No, I need you to teach me more Swahili."

"She'd refuse, folding her arms like a defiant child."

"Ok Ok, here's one. 'It's not my cup of tea'." She repeated it and I told her the meaning.

"I like that one. More."

"If your number is up, then it means you're going to die." She looked at me, screwing her face up.

"Oh my god, I hope my number doesn't come up for a long time, and yours…" she said, inching closer, staring straight into my eyes. "…not long for your number." She said it how I would have said it – with deadpan expression.

We both cracked up laughing. A girl forty years younger with my sense of humour.

She didn't have to tell me how close she was to her mother, I could tell by her face and smile as she talked about her. She died of malaria when she was nine and with no dad around she took on the mothering role in the house, looking after her sisters and missed a lot of school. Guilt struck me as she spoke. I left England without vaccinations – another one of many crazy risks I took in Africa. Unlike me, her mother and a lot of Africans don't have the luxury of free vaccinations like us, so I did feel guilty about that. She also told me about her dream of meeting a rich man who was going to scoop her up in his arms and take her far away.

"Now Madam, here's what's going to happen to you. A white man is going to come over here and he's going to ask you to go back with him on holiday."

"Yeh, pigs fly," was another one she liked to say.

"Yeh, it'll happen, but before you do he has to marry you first."

"What?"

"Yep, because if you don't and you go over for a holiday, you won't want to leave and it will upset you having to come back."

She thought about it and started nodding. "Thank you, wise old man."

"Don't be cocky," I said, wagging my finger at her. She just laughed.

The next afternoon I waited for her in our usual place but she didn't turn up. The barman told me she left that morning with her German friend but the weird thing is she seemed to do this a lot, disappear and then pop up surprising me wherever I was.

Most evenings, I used to walk the beaches and visit the other hotels, talking to the staff. Certain ones I'd tip and they'd get me into their restaurant to eat, pretending I was a guest, and if I didn't feel like going back to my hotel they'd even sort me out with a room – usually on the condition I would have to be out early before the chambermaids started the rounds.

I got to know the staff and the hotels along the beach, and like most of Kenya, they weren't on mains sewerage. I found this out one night when the tanker arrived. Checking in and out of hotels at different times of the day and night I got to know that a tanker does the rounds at around three in the morning, when most of the guests are asleep, and empties the sceptic tank. The smell had woken me up many a morning.

One time I woke as the air conditioning pumped a putrid smell into my room. I jumped out of bed and turned the thing off and went straight to reception.

"What smell?" the bloke said.

"The smell in my room, I can't breathe in there." I got the impression these two blokes were as tired as me and couldn't give a toss. "You'll have to put me up in another room then."

"Oh, we can't do that," he said.

"Why's that then?"

"The porter's got the keys." I could smell a different kind of shit now and was getting irritable. "I tell you what I'll do, I'm going to sleep here on those two chairs. I'll push them together ok? And in the morning I'll have a word with your fucking manager."

I walked over in full view of the reception, linked four chairs together and prepared to bed down for the night. Ten or so minutes later, the night porter appears with keys and I get upgraded to a premium room on the other side of the hotel without that nasty smell. I never liked complaining but it was unbearable.

Hotel staff work long, hard hours for their wages which worked out on average at about £40 a month.

Waiters and bar staff got most of the tips, which is usual wherever you go in the world. These people make the most contact with holidaymakers so naturally they get a majority of the share but I felt sorry for people like the hotel gardeners in Kenya. They work long hard hours in the heat. One bloke in particular was the most hard working and conscientious I'd ever seen. I'd see him as early as six in the morning and he'd still be going at eight or nine in the evening. I used to see him cutting, shaping and sculpting hedges around the pool with shears that he was continually having to sharpen, and he put so much effort and pride into his work.

One time I sat looking away from the pool watching him cut a two-foot hedge, and after a while he left the shears on the hedge and walked away. This was my chance, so I got up, went over and put a two hundred bob note under his cutters and walked back to my seat. He came back, picked his shears from the hedge and did a double take at the money, putting the shears back down quickly as if he was hiding what he had just found. Where did that come from? He stood back, put one hand on his hip, stretching back slightly as though he'd hurt himself and then started stretching his back out, twisting his upper torso like he was limbering up looking around wondering where this money had come from. What do I do? Do I take the money? I read his expression. He then moved back to hedge, lifted his shears and whipped the money straight into his pocket. Thank you very much.

About twenty minutes later, he left the shears again and was gone for about an hour, which gave me the chance to do it again. This time he came back to the hedge with his boss, who was inspecting his work. They chatted, the gardener lifted the shears to carry on, with his boss looking on. Seeing another note, the gardener slammed his shears down as fast as he picked them up. He turned to his boss and started chatting, stalling for time with his back to the hedge, the sheers and his money, hoping his boss would leave him to it. The boss was now getting closer to the shears, patting the hedge with his hand. Time for me to move. I walked over to them. "Hello."

They both smiled, answering me at the same time.

"Eh, this man's done a good job here," I said, pointing at this perfectly manicured hedge. We all stood there admiring his work. "Hey, what's the name of that?" I pointed up to a tall lilac flowered tree which stood behind the hedge he was cutting. The gardener didn't answer. "What it is then? Come on, tell the gentleman," his boss said, putting him under pressure.

The gardener was getting fidgety and flustered. We both looked at him waiting for his answer. His eyes darted around looking, hoping for some inspiration but he kept shuffling on the spot, folding then unfolding his arm, frowning confused looking at the tree and then down to the shears. He seemed anxious. I could feel his desperation as I became another threat to his money.

"Come on, you must know this," the boss said, urging him to remember.

"It's ok, no problem," I said, "but there is something I need to mention though," and I took the boss away from the hedge. As I did, a quick glance back and I saw the gardener was clipping like a man possessed with the money safely in his pocket.

The next day I waited my turn at the pool bar.

"Excuse me, sir." The voice came from behind. The gardener stood behind me, smiling. "I know it. That tree you asked about… it's a Jacaranda tree."

I looked at him like I didn't care. I could see he was expecting more of a reaction from me.

I stooped over my tall glass on the bar and sucked Bacardi and Coke through a straw.

"No it's not," I said, peering up from my glass. "That tree I said… is a money tree." I walked away with my drink, still sucking the straw, turned back at the bar, winked and watched his face change to a massive grin. He got it and waved to me. "Thank you… thank you very much."

7. Dodgy Deals and a Matatu

I checked out of the hotel and spent the next few weeks at the place Del Boy had recommended. The Evening Guest Hotel charged five pounds a night, was clean, tidy and cheap. I spent the next few weeks visiting and using other hotels along the coast. I met up with Del Boy and Rodney a few times, had coffee, and it was this pair who introduced me to wacky baccy.

They always met me with glazed eyes and reeked of the stuff. I smoked a few with them but wasn't really into it like that, it just made me tired and gave me a headache.

It was while I was with them that I realised it wasn't just ornaments they sold. We were having a drink and this smart silver-suited man walked in and immediately caught Del Boy's eye, stopping him mid-sentence. He made his excuses and told us both he wouldn't be long and he'd see us later.

I couldn't hear the conversation as they stood by the door but it didn't last long and they both left together, leaving me sat there with Rodders – who it turns out was deaf – which was why Del Boy did all the talking every time. The penny dropped.

Ten minutes later and now unsure if he was coming back I stood up and signalled to Rodders I was leaving. I used the same shortcut they showed me earlier to get back to the main road and back to my hotel. As I cut between two buildings I caught a glimpse of Del Boy talking to two guys in a silver Mercedes which was parked up at the back of someone's yard. The same silver-suited bloke in the pub sat at the wheel with the door wide open and Del Boy stood in the doorway with one arm on the roof and the other on the door. I couldn't let this go without sussing out the situation. I managed to move close enough to the car's blind spot out of view of wing mirrors where I could see better. I bent down and pretended to fasten my sandals and looked up and saw Del Boy duck his head into the car for a minute or so then step back out of the car, making no secret of the bundle of passports he had in his hand. Maroon in colour with a shiny coat of arms was a dead giveaway. I carried on back, wondering what other things Del Boy was into.

Nothing is done about the beach boys for one simple reason. Money.

They are the much needed connection between holidaymakers, the police and the airports, which all involves corruption and money.

A few weeks later, I followed three beach boys acting a bit dodgy, two of them seemed to be forcing the other bloke off the beach. They took him by the arm and marched him to the side of a hotel out of view and beat him up. The two blokes changed back into smarts suits in the car and drove off. What was all that about? I never did know but that was just scratching the surface of what was really going on. It did make me think not to trust Del Boy and Rodney.

I wanted every day in Kenya to be different from the next, and it was. Meeting people for the first time nearly always involved an invitation. A chat over coffee or a beer was followed by a guided tour around their house or land and to meet their family. I never said no and was always genuinely interested to see how they lived. Most had very little but what they did have they worked very hard for and were very proud to show me.

Three months had passed and it still felt like I was on an extended holiday but I soon realised I needed a job because my savings were fast running out. The cost of using taxis every day was mounting up and even though the place I was staying at was cheap I needed to save a bit of money so I stopped using taxis and took my chances in a Matatu.

A Matatu is a 'hop on, hop off' form of public transport. It's normally a minibus but I've seen all sorts used; flatbed trucks, lorries, vans – if it's got four or even three wheels and moves, they use it. Most would be unfit for our roads and you get a real sense of how crammed they are when one passes you by with a tied tower of luggage on the roof, swaying and bodies flapping, hanging off the back doors. No timetable. The driver leaves when it's physically impossible to get anyone else on it. If you didn't mind all that, it was a cheap way of getting around. Sometimes I'd stay on the thing and end up in the middle of nowhere and to places where I was the only white face. I did this a lot and there were times when I panicked, feeling anxious that I was being followed. When this happened, I just stayed on it to see how far it went.

The Matatus operated from Mombasa but connected all the remote villages with the city. One day I ended up on an old rundown industrial estate, miles from anywhere. I waited at a terminal as people seemed to appear from nowhere and the thing would fill again and we'd head back into the city.

I'd go as far down the coast as possible to where the coast comes to a dead end and would sit down for a chat with the driver and listen to the local gossip. I got talking to a driver called James; he was married with two kids and lived the other side of Mombasa. He told me business is tough. More and more families started their own Matatu business and with more on the road there were only so many customers to go around. He worked for someone else and had a daily target of people to pick up and said it was what made the job so dangerous. Speeding Matatus on the road cause a lot of accidents. Most work on commission – more pick-ups, more money and that's why they go as fast as possible so they pick up the next load of passengers. If you're lucky enough not to be involved in an accident you have to watch for police - even if you're not speeding they will look for any excuse to pull you over and if you're arrested you lose your daily target and your job with it. The best thing to do, he said, in that situation is pay the bribe the police want and get back on the road as quickly as possible. He earned an average of a thousand bob a week (£10) but his income wasn't fixed and depended on the how the day ended – the more passengers the more commission.

At some places I would get off the Matatu and kids would race up to me, squabbling for my attention.

"Eh mister, you want coconut?" and the next thing this little kid would scamper up the tree like a squirrel and bring down a coconut for a few bob.

I also got talking to fishermen who were mending their nets and their kids were playing football with a ball they made themselves from plastic bags bound together with elastic bands. On one occasion they let me join in.

"Look, the best place for me to go is the goal, ok?" I told them. "I'm old and slow." Big mistake that. They could really whack that ball at you.

One day, the Matatu picked me up and I stayed on as usual. We ended up out in the sticks again to another meeting place where people from remote areas gathered to pick up the newspapers or needed a lift, but mostly stood around gossiping. There was a crowd of about ten lads.

I asked the driver and he told me it was safe to get out. They all approached me and seemed surprised to see me. I picked out the ringleader even before he spoke. He was dressed a little bit neater than his scruffy-looking mates.

"Mzungu." This is your first time in Kenya, isn't it?" I could hear the cockiness as he spoke and his mates listened on.

"Yes," I said. "This is my first time in Kenya. It's my first holiday and I've got on this to see how far it went."

"Ok...just to let you know we are very poor people and I'd like to take you over to see my house in minute. Is that ok?"

"Ok, how far is it?"

"Not far," he said and turned to walk, signalling me to follow.

"I have a question for you first," I said, stopping him dead.

"Has your house got a tin roof?" He nodded. "Don't tell me," I said, raising my hand. "You have one or two rooms and instead of wallpaper you've got pieces of newspaper, magazine cuttings, footballers' pictures stuck everywhere. You pay about ten or twenty pounds a month rent?"

Now his face was dropping and the other smaller boys were lighting up with smiles.

"Looking at your build I guess you make your money pushing that fucking water cart back and forth to Mombasa seven drums at a time, and the reason you want me to go over to the village to show me the house, is to con me. You will show me somebody else's house, one with a dirty mattress, is that right?" The boys were getting noisy and started to cheer and clap, including my Matatu driver.

"He's got you there, you've picked on the wrong bloke, he knows more than you." He looked uncomfortable but took it all in good part and before I left I gave him a few hundred bob. "Here you are, stay away from the Changaa."

This was first of many scams I came across. It wasn't a bad scam really, these lads were trying to make a buck, but to them I was an old, white and gullible tourist, walking around alone on their land, which made me a target. The driver knew these lads and that reassured me a bit that I could have a bit fun with them. The Matatu drivers were a good source of local knowledge and gave me advice on where not to go, but my biggest problem was when I went walking on my own.

8. Poking My Nose In

My 'poking my nose in' habit was getting worse. It got me into all sorts of trouble. Like the time in Likoni when I drifted into one of the shanty back streets just up the hill from the Ferry.

It was six something in the morning and most places were closed but I came across a bar and could hear voices so I pushed the door, thinking it was locked but it wasn't and in I strolled.

I tried to ignore the blokes who were massive and seemed to grow like trees from their seats as they stood up, staring at me. Trying to give myself a reason as to why I was there I thought of coffee and reached down for my bumbag. Without looking directly at them, I could feel their stare on me and realised by the circle of chairs in the middle of the room that I had interrupted their meeting. I also clocked a couple of guys sat near the door which I was now too far away from using without being challenged. Fuck. No-one spoke. Kenyans are normally a friendly bunch, especially with tourists, but something told me, an instinct maybe that this was one place I shouldn't be. I sensed these guys weren't going to show me around their houses and if they did, would I survive the experience? I had to do something, and quick.

"I've been robbed," I said, then repeated it louder. "I've been robbed." I moved my hand down to the bum bag on my hip, quickly unzipping and turning the pouch inside out, pointing to it. "They've taken all my money, my passport, everything." I slumped down onto the nearest chair, looking sorry for myself, and as I did I saw money in piles on the table. My guess is these guys had been busy in the night and were now sharing the profit. The guys looked as bewildered as I was trying look myself. What was this old white guy doing around here at this time of day?

"Go to the police," one said.

The silence seemed to last for ages, so it was nice to hear a voice, especially constructive advice, because the atmosphere was freaking me out. I just didn't know what these guys were going to do next.

Continuing to act out the scene, I replied, "No money, look." I showed them all the bottom of my bum bag again.

Chair legs scraped the floor as one bloke sprawled over the table scooping the money together with both hands. Another guy stood up, grabbed my arm before speaking, which scared the shit out of me.

"Come with me." This mountain of a bloke walked me up to the main road and we found his mate, a taxi driver and explained my situation. That is how I got out of that place. My gut instinct, which I started to use more and more, told me I was in the wrong place and definitely at the wrong time, and I didn't want to take any chances so I reacted before they could. My 'harmless old man' routine, my 'just been mugged' routine had done the trick.

After being robbed in Barclays I made sure I never carried a lot of cash, normally just a few Kenyan pounds for a taxi and something to eat. The evening before gate- crashing those blokes I'd changed rooms, cleared the deposit box and put everything I had including my passport in my bum bag and forgot about it. I first realised this in the bar when I felt a thick wad in my bumbag. Luckily, it has two compartments; of course I showed them the empty one.

Meeting them that morning should have taught me a lesson, but it didn't. I carried on poking my nose in, and if the situation was dangerous then it added to the thrill of the experience.

The next dangerous situation I got involved in was when I changed some money. The reps at the hotel always advise holidaymakers not to exchange money in the street for obvious reasons. I'd heard different stories about how holidaymakers were conned out of their money and I was intrigued to know how it was done so I went into Mombasa to find out.

Moi Avenue is famous for two aluminium elephant tusks that cross the dual carriageway. It was built in honour of Princess Margaret's visit to the city in the fifties. I started my search at the tusk end and casually walked down the Avenue, passing a few taxi drivers who were in and out of their cars, talking and waiting for their next fare. I even saw one driver with two holidaymakers exchanging money but I sensed this was a normal transaction. These weren't conmen, this was just a side-line for them and they would charge five per cent more than the bank rate, which included a bit of cheeky banter. I carried on walking and saw my target; he stood out being smartly suited with shiny patent leather shoes. He was leant over, buffing, polishing up the roof of his car. He wasn't putting a lot of effort into the job in hand, just gently swiping the car with his cloth, looking around every few seconds. As I walked past him, I knew he would talk to me, and he did. He took a final glance around before he spoke. "Hey mate, you want to change money?"

"No, I've only got twenty dollars."

"That's ok, I can change it, I get you a very good rate."

"No, it's ok." I was still unsure of whether to see this through. I walked away and watched the man move away from his car, now standing opposite a block of flats. I went back over to him.

"Ok, I've only got twenty dollars but I do need the best price."

"Follow me, my mate's got a shop."

So I did. We crossed the road and went into the flats through a wide entrance, turning left and went up three or four steps into a darkened area of the building and I was made to wait on a wide terrace. "You stay here, I get my mate," and he disappeared. Now this feels dangerous, I thought. Two men return, his mate lifts up a plastic ID badge chained around his neck. I couldn't see a face on it, just a black smudge. It could have been anyone. I handed over the money and that was it. I didn't see them again. I'm still standing there when I hear a neighbour's door open. "Hey Mister, those men are conmen from Nairobi."

I turned around and I could see part of his face through the gap of the chained door.

"Yeh, I know," I said, turning my back on him. He watched me take out my laser pen and shine the beam down the corridor. "It's not my money, but I've got the photographs."

"You CIA?" he asked.

"Yep." I flicked the end of the pen off, put it back in my pocket and walked away.

I took a risk, maybe to others a big risk. I tried to minimise the risk and thought things through first. My appearance; I wore tatty sandals, shorts and t-shirt. No jewellery and I made a point of telling the first guy I only had twenty dollars which was enough to get his mate out of bed but not enough to kill me. Of course I didn't chase them and put up a fight because they probably would have hurt me or even killed me. This scam really works for them when they find a stupid tourist who has got money, jewellery, etc. and no choice but to give them the lot.

It was a dangerous way of finding things out but it satisfied my curiosity. I started to go into Mombasa a lot after that and would spend hours talking to the taxi drivers on Moi Avenue. They sat on boxes, crates buckets, anything they could turn upside down and use for a seat, and we'd sit around and chat.

There was a lad in his twenties who used to trawl up and down Moi Avenue selling stuff to the tourists. One day, he came up to me, pushing his bike and asked me if I wanted to buy it.

"Your bike, yeh right. Come on, whose is it? Who did you nick it off?"

He just grinned at me. "You want to ride it for the day?"

"Come on then, let's have a little spin on it." So I climbed on and pedalled away. I'd not been on a bike for a while and he laughed as I wobbled away until I steadied myself and circled around a few times. I wasn't too far from the main Momba-sa/Nairobi highway when a big heavy lorry crawled along with black smoke billowing from it and the load of timber it was carrying was slipping away from the back. One of the rear wheels was shredded and on fire. The driver kept going at about five miles per hour and suddenly stopped further up the road. He jumped down, leaving the lorry standing blocking the middle of road and was now running at me with a trailing roll of cloakroom raffle tickets in one hand and was waving at me with the other. I manoeuvred the bike around with the pedal up, poised to move quickly at any moment from this mad bloke coming my way.

"A pound each," he shouted at me.

The flames and acrid black smoke billowed from the back end, creating a smog all around his lorry, causing other cars to swerve around it and all he wanted to do was sell me a raffle ticket – only in Kenya.

I rode the bike back to the lad. "What was all that about?" he said.

"Dunno, must have been a bloody relative of yours. Anyway, here's fifty bob for riding your bike." At that moment, a Matatu was closing in on us and his mate jumped out and put the bike on the roof and I jumped on with them.

Another time I was talking to the drivers about the fares and tips they got. My driver pointed out this bloke who never tipped, who was Dutch and in his early forties, talking to one of the other drivers. He had a long scar running down the side of his neck and was telling anybody that listened about his accident, recounting his story and mentioning his £100,000 insurance payout.

I thought he was either full of shit or stupid, or both. Stupid because if it was true he was asking for trouble by telling everyone about his money. He was staying just around the corner and paying next to nothing for very basic accommodation – a small single room which had access to cooking facilities.

I tried slipping away from the drivers without Dutch seeing me but he caught me up, telling me about his collection of airline blankets.

"What do you want those for?" I asked him.

Every time he flew he waited for the plane to empty and moved through the row of seats collecting these thin blue blankets issued free of charge to passengers.

"Shorts."

"Shorts?"

"Yeh shorts. I take them to a woman in Mombasa and she makes them into shorts for me, made to measure for fifty pence. Fifty pence," he said again, holding five fingers up as if I couldn't count. He was chuffed I could tell.

A hundred grand in the bank, staying at the roughest B&B in the city, shorts made from free airport blankets. This was one tight fucker. I thought that was taking austerity measures a bit too far.

I made my excuse and left him to it. I told him I had to see one of the drivers and doubled back around to the taxis and told them all about the Dutch man and his shorts. They all cracked up laughing, especially when I told them what they were made from.

The 29th of January, my fifty-seventh birthday and I decided I wanted to spent the day back in Likoni. I went back to see Sharon and the bar where we first met. "It's my birthday today," I announced to the Landlord and Sharon's family and friends. More and more people started to come over and talk to me, congratulating me. "Right," I said, rubbing my hands together. It's your birthday as well, tonight we all eat together. Now then, I want rice for twenty, no, say forty because I'm sure we'll get others." I knew the price of rice but I didn't have a clue about goat. "Here's seven hundred bob (£7)." I gave it to the Landlord. "Now I don't want to get ripped off so make sure you get me a nice one. More than likely he'll get one for four hundred and he'll make on the rest but anyway I sent him off. "

I left them all to it and came back when it was almost dark, but there was no sign of the goat. All the women were gathered around cooking the rice and the Landlord must have picked up some cheap booze because they were all sipping and stirring the pots. Half an hour later, still no goat. So I was thinking I'd been well and truly ripped off when along came these two kids, about six years old, pulling a stroppy-looking goat. The Landlord appears at the same time.

"Eh, I was expecting the goat to be dead."

"No problem," he said.

He took a knife and lifted the goat, grabbing it's neck and slicing it's throat and within a few minutes the poor old goat was in the boiling pot, cooking away.

Now time for fun. I took out my laser pen. They were popular in the UK at the time but no one had seen one here before. The kids were entranced by it and followed me and my beam around in the dark; they thought I was some sort of magician. I walked over to a neighbour's house and shone the pen through a slatted fenced to where the cockerels lived and they started chasing the dot which I kept moving around the yard. The kids howled with laughter at these birds going mental running around in circles bumping into each other, one ending up crashing into the fence. I quickly put the pen away and we all moved away quickly as the neighbour came, wondering what all the noise was about.

My party went on into the early hours of the morning and others villagers came out to share the leftovers and we all sat around the glowing embers of the fire, laughing and joking under the stars. It was a magical night.

The next morning, with my head feeling a bit fuzzy, I went down the shop. The shop was a shack on the side of the road. It sold lots of individual items which were laid on shelving at the front or pinned up on the wall.

I used to like getting up early in the mornings before anyone was around and cross over to the village see the old shopkeeper; in the end we got to know each other. We used to chat and I would see who turned up and what they bought for breakfast. Most couldn't afford to eat and just had a tea or coffee.

A bony little girl of about six came in and asked for two cigarettes and fours spoons of tea.

"What you having for breakfast, love?"

"Tea."

"A cup of tea?" I said.

She gave me a big nod back. I thought her little head was gonna fall off. I winked at the old boy passing him money and a list at the same time as he was scooping tea into a small bag. Now her order had expanded to a full shopping bag which she was never going to carry.

"How far do you live, love?"

"Not far."

So I walked over with her, carrying this bag which I handed her back, leaving her to go into this little hut. I hid nearby and listened.

"Where did you get all this from?" her mum said as she emptied the bag. Bread, milk, potatoes.

"A mzungu. A mzungu gave it to me at the shop." The next minute the door opened and they both came out looking for me, but I was well-hidden and waited till they went back in before I went back to the shop.

9. Flying Cats and Drug Smuggling

On another morning, at about five or six o'clock, I did my usual walkabout thing in the village as they started their day. People loaded vehicles and carts, stacking them high and shops and bars were being cleaned. I could hear cats screaming so I followed the noise, which got louder, and it seemed to come from a bar with tables and chairs stacked outside. As I stepped up into the doorway, something flew by me, splattering me with something wet as it went by. I looked down to see red patches of blood on my shirt and then to the furry dead thing in the road. The next thing I know, another cat is flying past me, this time I got right out of the way and it landed near the other one. I waited before going in, looking down, I saw another one darting out of the doorway, scurrying away with its life, followed by a blood covered broom which was chasing it. I made the bloke holding it jump as I was the last person he expected to see after executing two cats. He looked shocked and embarrassed as I pulled at my shirt, showing him splatters of blood.

"I don't like cats," was all he said, then went back in and closed the door.

Now I've never been a big pet lover but I was appalled to see these poor battered cats fly past me. I walked away feeling a bit numb. Throughout my time in Kenya I couldn't get the image of those dead cats slumped in the road out of my head. It really had an effect on me.

For most Kenyan families, keeping a pet is an extra expense and not a high priority and the main reason hotels keep domestic cats is to control vermin and they also know how much of a soft spot us Brits have for pets. Wherever I stayed, cats were allowed to appear at meal times and roam around the outside tables so holidaymakers would feed them.

With money now running out, I needed to get a job to keep my African adventure going. I didn't have a clue what but I knew I had to get something sorted and soon. Realistically, my chances weren't good. How could I come to a third world country and expect to work. I found out the only foreigners who lived and worked in Kenya were the rich ones, the ones who had money to start with and owned the luxury lodges, pampering the rich holidaymakers on safari. I realised I was naive to think I could make money and worried about what I would do when my money ran out. I also wanted to send money to Ann to help her out because I knew she would struggle. Then I began to think of other ways of making money and the thought of me smoking wacky backy with the beach boys gave me the idea.

I knew a few lads in England who smoked and sold it, so that was handy. I was never going to be a major drugs baron but as long as I had enough to stay in Kenya and send a bit to Ann, then I was happy.

The following night, Del Boy and Rodney turned up at my hotel with two kilos of grass, a roll of cling film in a crumpled plastic shopping bag, tattered and torn. I opened the bag, took out the dark package which was stretched tight in cling film, piercing it open by pushing two fingers in and pinched a bit out, inhaling it under my nose. I didn't have a clue but I wanted to give the impression I did. I wasn't going to get ripped off.

"How much then?"

"A hundred pounds sterling."

I laughed. "Come on, you can do better than that."

"No, this is the best," and he went on to explain how good it was.

I'm not getting ripped off, I thought. I took out sixty quid from my wallet and handed it to them. "Here, and this is all I can give, ok?"

They both looked at each and nodded and my first drug deal was done. When they left me to it, I had to open all the windows because this stuff stank and started to make the room smell, so I quickly wrapped it back up with the cling film.

I moved onto the tiled floor in the bathroom and mummified the package in thirty metres of cling film, adding a splash of bleach toilet cleaner to each layer. I thought against wearing gloves, they would just transfer the smell around and those sniffer dogs at the airport would pick up the scent. I was better off scrubbing my hands with soap several times throughout the whole process.

I looked at the wrapped package and couldn't help thinking I'd made a mistake already – a mistake involving Del Boy – risky, especially knowing he was up to all sorts of shit and I got the feeling he would supply his mother's body parts for cash, but I was desperate to make this work so I could stay in Africa.

If there was going to be a second time, I wouldn't use the beach boys again. I needed to source my own contacts. It wouldn't be easy but I was sure I would feel less anxious about taking two kilos through two airports than I did at that time.

I didn't get much sleep that night, I couldn't stop thinking about airports and sniffer dogs.

I looked at the package again in the morning and wondered if it needed a few more layers and kept picking it up, holding and sniffing it to see what I could smell. I packed, then repacked my suitcase and felt nervous, shaking inside and I hadn't even left the hotel. That feeling got worse in the cab and when I clapped eyes on the airport, I was almost sick on the spot. I started to evaluate what I was doing, my mind forcing me to question my judgement. The money. Terry, the money, think about the money. Is it worth the risk? Can you stay in Kenya without money? No. Are you living your dream? Yes. Do you want your dream to end? No. And that was enough to convince me to see this through.

Drug crime equals ten years in prison – don't do it. The sign as I entered the airport should have been enough for me to turn around and walk back out, but I kept on walking, doing my best to think of anything but that sign.

Paranoid, now thinking everyone knew what I was up to, that moment the conveyor took my case after being weighed and tagged, was the worst feeling. That was it, no turning back. My mouth was awash with sourness, the bile rising. I hurried, following the sign for the toilets, keeping my mouth tightly closed. I marched into a cubicle, just about locking the door before spewing. The same feeling continued when I got to departures. I was alone with my own voice in my head that was trying to calm me down but just couldn't relax. My head was all over the place. Fear and panic gripped me – it felt like everybody was watching me.

Most people at an airport do the duty free shops thing and then find their spot until the gate opens.

I moved around erratically and indecisively; sitting, standing, then sitting again. I browsed the same duty free shops, pretending to show interest. I wore a thick cotton shirt which just made me constantly sweat, making me even more self-conscious. I was acting like drug smuggler, not at all discreet and if anyone official-looking had spoken to me I would have got caught.

Heathrow was a tense affair too, waiting for my case and waiting to be caught. I got far enough away from the main doors at Heathrow, jumped in a cab and the moment it pulled away I could feel my body loosen as I relaxed back into the seat. I had been holding my breath for the last twelve hours and could now breathe.

I reflected, replaying that day a lot and realised if I was going to be any good at this drug smuggling, then I needed to get a grip and I had a plan.

The trip back to Kenya would obviously be drug free so I decided to tune in to how that felt. I monitored my own behaviour of being relaxed, what I did for those few hours and why I did them and how others perceived me. The objective of this exercise was to hold on to this memory and recall it, visualising myself at that point. I did it the next trip and every time afterwards, the more I did it the more I felt invincible. I slowly became a very accomplished drug smuggler. I also prepared a strategy for when I was challenged and practised in the mirror what I would say and how I would say it and how I looked saying it. I even practised with my arm fully extended, holding a passport as still as I possibly could. No shakes, no drugs, was my motto on that one.

10. Airport Stories

My plan worked. After a few more trips I didn't even need to do the visualising again; it became second nature, but that said I nearly got caught on another trip all because I didn't read my ticket properly.

Everything about that flight was fine until the announcement woke me up and told me to fasten my seat belt. I checked my watch. Too early for Heathrow. I could have asked anyone but I waited for the stewardess who was working her way through the plane, checking seat belts and floor space for obstructions.

Amsterdam, she told me and asked me where I was going. I told her and she advised me to stay on board as the plane would only be re-fuelling and then would carry on to Heathrow.

This was trip number six and I was ready for any situation, which was just as well.

I became an expert under pressure. It was before 9/11 and I realised airport security couldn't check every bag all of the time and they depended on watching people under pressure to see how they reacted. Today I played the part of a weary old traveller at Heathrow and sat away from the crowd who were all jostling for position at the carousel. I sat slouched against my hand luggage and duty free fags with my face propped up by my elbow. I even threw in a few yawns to give the impression that I was in no rush unlike the rest to get my case.

Slowly, the crowd began to thin as people collected their luggage and made their way to Passport Control. Large gaps appeared between the cases left on the carousel until eventually thinning down to just three and that 'first trip quivering sickness' feeling hit my stomach again. It was the same three cases parading around so I knew I was in trouble.

The last three moved forward in turn and grabbed their cases, leaving the carousel empty, which did a few more laps, finally jolting to a stop. No more luggage. I waited, hoping for the machine to spring back to life but it didn't.

Fuck. Fuck. Fuck. They must have my case. It's all over.

Then I remembered details about my flight, I bought a cheaper ticket this time around, which involved me changing planes at Amsterdam. That's it Terry, you should have got off the plane. I should have got off that fucking plane. I didn't but my case did. Now what? Run for it? What do I do? My head was busy.

I needed to think and I needed a fag. Ten hours without one for someone who has smoked for forty-five years is too long. Security unlocked the door to the smoking terrace and told me to buzz the intercom to come back in. I stood alone in the dark and smoked one then another and came to the only conclusion. I took a few deep breaths and buzzed myself back in and walked straight over to the desk. A short stubby woman with a satsuma fake tan, painted with lots of bright make up responded to the bell.

"Oh hello, my name is Johnson, I've just—"

"Mr T Johnson," she announced.

"Terry, yeh that's right."

"We've been waiting for you, Mr Johnson."

'Mr Johnson'. She repeated my name so I dreaded the worst. "You landed at Amsterdam, didn't you?"

I nodded.

"Why didn't you get off the plane like your ticket told you to?" I didn't bother explaining, I got the feeling she had something to tell me. She spoke slower now, adding more drama to the situation. "You didn't get off, but your luggage did and when it did without you, it caused a major security alert – they thought it was a bomb." She paused then smiled. "It's all ok now. Everything is fine, after a few checks we were able to trace you and knew you would be here waiting for your case, so panic over."

My case was on the next flight due in three hours' time and she told me to stay around and collect it from the small carousel alongside the desk. I tried to summarise events in my head and come to some kind of conclusion.

Apart from the ticking off from Tango lady, everything seemed to be fine. What was happening here? Was it a delaying tactic? Did they need me to claim the bag before arresting me? The thought of doing a runner came back to me.

I spent the next three hours sat drinking coffee, watching the cleaners. Hazard cones marked out the areas they were cleaning. I was tired and found it almost hypnotic watching the speed of their mops moving side to side, towing their yellow wheeled buckets behind. It was the longest three hours of my life. I was still doubting my decision to hang around, waiting for the arrivals board to change, and when it did I got up, went back to the desk and waited. The only noise in the airport came from a stag party at the other end which seemed to echo through the place and then it happened. Whoosh, the carousel burst into life, I watched, waiting for movement behind the dangling strips of plastic. Then it appeared – my case. I knew straight away it was mine, day glow green taped handles with a carved wooden giraffe pendant. The case moved towards me and then the machine stopped, silence again, it felt eerie; just me and my case. I stood trying to make sense of it all. Am I at this second being watched? I braced myself, fearing the worst, a voice or a hand on my shoulder. I gripped the handle and heaved it onto the trolley and pushed it to the exit. Automatic doors opened and the chilly air hit my face as I got into the nearest taxi.

"Coach terminal please."

I looked back at the airport as we pulled away. A bomb scare, security alert at an international airport and never once did they check my case. How the hell did I get away with that?

Most people use the first few seconds to judge a person or a situation and base their decision on that, especially at airports where time and delays are a factor.

Looking back I was lucky my new career was before the increase in security from the events of 9/11 but even so, there were times when if I reacted differently I'm sure I would have been caught. Confidence is the key and what you do and say in those few seconds is the difference. The more I did it, the better I became.

In the late nineties, before you entered Mombasa Airport, you had to leave your case on the paved area just outside the main entrance, show your passport, and your case was taken and put through the x-ray machine just inside the door.

It was early morning when I showed the guy my passport and could see the x-ray area was fairly empty and four young Kenyans were waiting keenly for luggage.

"Put it on...put it on," the guy ordered.

I did and I moved slowly into position at the other end and waited until my case reappeared. As it did, I grabbed the handle.

"Wait a minute." I looked up. The guy spoke behind the monitor. "What's this?" I walked over for a closer look.

It was an x-ray outline of my bag. "What is this?" He left his finger tapping at the dark shape on the screen.

"Jambo Habari," I said without hesitation. Intrigued, the other guys surrounded the monitor too.

"What?"

"Jambo Habari. I bought it from the beach boys. It's carved from black mahogany into the words *Jambo Habari*".

"What do you want that for?" he snapped back at me, searching my face for an answer.

"I'm going to put it on my bathroom door."

They carried on studying the image in silence; one of the guys was moving his finger across the screen explaining something.

"Right, stay there," not sure why I said that because they had no intention of moving. "I'll open it, I'll show you." I went back to my case, heaved it down off the machine, and as I did I noticed a bit of a queue behind me so I took my time unlocking the padlock.

"No, no. It's ok. Go on," and abruptly waved his hand at me. It worked.

I walked away with the greatest urge to look back at those guys. They weren't entirely convinced but I sold them my confidence and it worked. I reckon they were watching me, waiting for my reaction and I had an unbelievable urge to look back but I knew that would be a mistake.

Once, I landed in Gatwick and couldn't afford a hotel so I stayed in the airport for the night. The plan was to get the early morning coach home. I sat and dozed off then woke to the sight of police approaching. Two armed coppers walked towards me with machine guns strapped across their chest, one holding the lead of a rusty brown and white cocker spaniel.

"Evening sir. Nice tan."

They stopped for a chat and I told them where I'd been and it turned out that one of them was getting married there so I gave him some tips.

Now bored with our conversation, the dog moves closer to the case, decides to rest its chin on the end of it and then closes its eyes, oblivious to the three kilos inside. I didn't know if the dog was a trained sniffer, even so, for that dog to be so close to the drugs was nerve-wracking but I kept it together and they left me alone to sleep. I was mad to stay anywhere in the airport but I had no choice – it was another close call.

11. That's my Boy

I spent several years going backwards and forwards, taking all sorts of risks along the way and getting away with them. I got distracted with the whole drug smuggling and it wasn't until a few years later that I went back to Likoni. I don't know why I left it so long, I guess I had other places to discover. It was before mobile phones so I relied on Sharon's post box number to let her know when and where to meet her, and I suggested a cafe that she knew well.

I had no photos of her so it could have been anyone turning up to see me. I sat outside a cafe in Likoni and waited for her. She crossed the road, calling my name and then hugged me. She looked down as she spoke to the little boy holding her hand. First thing I noticed was the colour of his skin – much lighter than his mum's. She was from the northern tribe, very dark and he was slightly darker than me but he did look familiar.

We sat and drank coffee and I quickly came to terms with my shock. A new son at my age. She explained she'd had no way of contacting me, so had desperately waited to hear from me every day, hoping to get post from me, and when she did, she knew this would be a lot for me to take in. I told her not to worry and would send money every month and visit the village to see him, and not once every four years, which she was relieved about.

I spent the next few days with my new family, getting to know my son, and I made a big fuss over him. He didn't speak English but that wasn't a problem – we communicated by pulling stupid faces and clowning about and he took to me very quickly. I took him for his first ever ice cream. I watched his reaction as I gave him the cornet; he stared at it, and instead of licking it he tried biting instead and then screwed his face up with ice cold shock. "Look," I said, "watch me." I bent down with my ice cream so he could see me.

He watched me lick mine and then it was his turn. Carefully, he moved his little tongue slowly to the ice cream, afraid of what would happen, but then he tasted the ice cream properly and smiled up at me as he carried on devouring it. I took him swimming and, for a toddler, he was very athletic and used to stand on my shoulders and leap off; he was fearless.

Every time I came back, I used the last few days of my holiday to see my new son. His mother always seemed to want us to meet up and spend the day on quiet beaches along the coast.

12. Scousers and Yanks

I spent the next few months smuggling drugs through Heathrow and Gatwick Airports and getting ripped off trying to sell it. I didn't really know the value and I didn't really care as long as it made me enough to live in Kenya. It was never going to make me rich.

Up till now I had always stuck to the south coast hotels but I did try the north. I stayed at the Bamburi Beach Hotel and noticed at breakfast how empty it was. The Safari was the reason. The waiter told me he was up at four o'clock in the morning, making cups of tea for the guests who left for the Safari. Most of the guests at the hotel were my age and older, especially the big party of twenty-three from Colchester who were all in their mid-seventies.

I finished breakfast and went down to the beach wall and looked around, still surprised by the lack of people. The beach boys knew the check-in times at most hotels and would hang over the wall on the beach side where they could shout and tempt the new guests onto the beach to buy something. But even they weren't around and that was odd.

"There's a purge on, you won't see them today," said the groundsman. "They owe the authorities money so the beaches are patrolled looking for them, they're too frightened to come out."

I decided to sit with a coffee in the foyer; it was nice and cool there, looking out through the glass at the front entrance, watching the reaction of the new guests arriving. A few private taxis rolled up and staff gathered outside with a suitcase trolley, ready to pounce and open doors when needed.

Then a coach pulled up and a load of blokes got off. I recognised their accents straight away – scousers. About thirty of them in their twenties.

They stepped off the coach like bears coming out from hibernation, stretching, yawning, rubbing eyes as staff unloaded and lined up the cases. They suddenly came alive, getting louder as they all realised their holiday was about to begin. They fidgeted, pacing around reception impatient to check-in and sign paperwork. All they wanted to do was to get down to the bar and a few were drawn to the window taking in the beach and the Indian Ocean.

They all returned a bit later and sat at the bar and one bloke got my attention by leaning back on his stool. "Eh mate, is this hotel always like this?"

I sipped and nodded. "Yep, I'm surprised to see you lads here. This place is for old bastards like me." They all laughed and I moved closer to chat. I told them I travelled alone and came to Kenya quite a lot, which they thought was cool. The lads were on a two-week stag holiday and the groom was now dressed in a pink tutu.

Another gang of pensioners had gathered nearby and were listening to the rep as she explained all about the hotel.

One of the reasons I chose the north coast was because I knew Madam would be staying here the whole season; she told me the place to go to if I needed to find her. I didn't need to because she had this knack of just turning up wherever I was and used the beach boys to search me out. A week into my stay and I was surprised that I hadn't seen her. I did think of looking for her but I was in no rush – I knew at some point we would meet.

I was normally one of the first in for dinner but these lads beat me to it. They weren't interested in dressing for dinner, just eating, and they piled their plates up high. They'd spent the day drinking and were now stuffing themselves. I sat a few tables away but could hear the argument getting louder about whose round it was. It wasn't all-inclusive back then and the hotel seemed fairly expensive compared to the bars around the coast which were nearly half the price.

I bided my time and waited for them to talk me again, and it wasn't long before one of them came over. "Hi mate, is there any fucking nightlife round here or what?" The others gathered around my table to listen.

"Yeh plenty, just let me know when you wanna change the scenery, ok?"

"Now," he pleaded, "right now, this place is a fucking morgue," he said.

"Let me finish this and I'll meet you at reception in ten minutes."

They followed me out of the rear of the hotel. I heard a few whispers. I guessed they wondered where an old fogie like me would take them.

"Where we goin'?"

"Down to the beach. Follow me."

"Fuck me, it's dark down there," he said.

They sensed excitement and were in high spirits, laughing and joking, making a lot of noise. I led them along the beach and the lights of our hotel became distant with a big patch of darkness in between each bar that we passed. I looked at each one to check and found the one I was looking for. We came to a concrete ramp into another complex and an outside bar surrounded with sand and platform for dancing and loads of tables and chairs.

I was told this place was the liveliest on the beach. It didn't look like it.

"Look lads, this is the place."

"What's that for?"

"That's a dance floor, ya prat."

"Yeh, but who we going to dance with?"

"I don't fucking fancy dancing with this lot," he nodded around to couples sat in twos with a lit candle between them on each table.

"Well let's see what happens a bit later on, eh?" I kept my tone of voice mysterious and they went along with it.

The noise these lads were making on the beach I was certain she was going to show up. A bit later I left them at the bar and walked over to the nearest outside toilets at the side of the hotel, and by chance I saw a tall, statuesque shadow through the bushes near the front area of the next hotel along.

She circled a small area, looking at the road and then looked down to us at the beach, saw me, then waved. It was her. The lads moved from the bar and were now lined along the sand, facing up to the dance floor and the metal frame of lights flashing different colours. The lads were holding and swigging their beer, unaware of what I could see. They were a bit muted and docile, now sensing how shit their night was going to be, and just nodding their heads back and forwards in time with the music. The DJ did his best cranking the music up and it didn't take long for the couples to pay up and leave. I positioned my self at an angle where the lads could see me and where I could also see the toilets; she waved at me and the next minute she was running down the beach towards me with Cher's 'Do you believe in love?' booming from the speakers. I got the lads' attention and they all watched as this crazy girl charged at me at speed, leaping in the air, folding her long legs up into a cradle position, instinctively I held my arms out and caught her.

They all whistled, cheered and clapped and circled us, still clutching their bottles, questioning me.

"Eh, who's this then?" They all went quiet and wanted to know who this young twenty-year old girl was who appeared from nowhere for this old man. I started to explain as seriously as I could.

"Well, it's a bit sad really, she s got a problem with her head, you know." I turned my head away from her, tapped my temple and mouthed, "She's a bit mental" at them.

"Yeh, she thinks I'm nineteen." They looked at one another, not sure what to think. "She can't speak English so it's ok." She kept quiet and went along with everything but I could feel her jabbing my ribs.

"I'm sorry to hear that, mate." Some smirked but he was serious.

She turned and winked at me so I knew she was up to something.

"I na haja," she said, walking away.

One lad overheard and asked if she was a Muslim. "I've heard that word before," he said.

"What, I na haja?"

"Yeh."

"It means 'I have a need, like go to the toilet, that's where she's gone."

Ten minutes later and I saw her at roughly the same point as before and walked over to her.

"How many?"

"About twenty."

"Well I've got sixty-five here," she said.

"Just give me the signal."

"Ok," and I walked back to the lads.

"They asked if I was ok."

"Yeh, no problem," I said.

These lads were itching for a good night and a few were knocking back the beer and getting ready to go back to the hotel, get a taxi and go into town.

"Eh, it's so fucking quiet, what's the point of all this music, there's no fucker 'ere."

Madam came over and stood in front of them and surprised some of them with her ability to speak English. (Her grasp of it put theirs to shame). As she was talking, a pack of girls were running, closing in behind them.

"Ok lads, you Liverpudlians, I've got some Beatles fans I want you to meet." As she finished talking, they didn't get the chance to fully turn around before the stampede jumped all over them. Crushing, flattening them to the ground, sending tables and chairs flying. It was mayhem. They picked one guy up, whether he was hurt or shocked or pissed, I wasn't sure, but they carried him off inside to lie down.

The lads were outnumbered three to one and the party started. They got their wish and it's fair to say their quiet night soon changed to a wild one.

The next day the scousers were having breakfast outside on the terrace.

"Where you been? Where's your friend, wife or whoever she is?"

"Madam? Ah, you won't see her again. Bringing her into the hotel for the day costs too much money. Unless she's with a guest, she won't be allowed in."

"Ahhh, we want to see you two together again, bring her in. Don't worry about the money, we'll sort that out, won't we lads?" They all nodded in agreement.

"Old man." We all looked around. Unbelievable timing as usual. She strode across from the beach, vaulted the wall, looking and checking for staff.

"Hello scousers," she said, parting the lads who were standing around the table and making a big fuss of me, wrapping her arms around me, parking herself on my lap.

One of the lads took me aside. "Look, we've had a whip around. We've got a hundred quid to give to her. Is that alright?"

"Certainly not." His face dropped at my reaction. "No. You can't give her a hundred pounds. Give her a fiver and I'll have the rest."

"What?"

"I'm only joking, you silly prat."

"I don't know when you're joking and when you're serious."

I went missing for the next few days. I did my normal thing; up first, mooching around and then heading out to Mombasa and returning late at night.

Some of the hotels along the coast have orphanages with collection points where holidaymakers can leave food or clothing. On certain days, the hotels arrange for you to go to these orphanages and show you around.

I wondered how I could do my bit. I've always been sceptical of how charities and people collecting for them worked, and I've been under the impression that someone somewhere is creaming off the donations. The longer I lived in Kenya, the more I found this to be the case. For example, charities encourage holidaymakers to donate pens and books to local schools. The hotel I was staying at had a glass case half full with biros and lined exercise books which regular visitors would top up. I visited a few schools in and around the area and saw no sign of these donated biros and books.

How could I help?

I did a chapati run – it was my bit to help and to make sure my donation got to those who needed it most. I found out that most of the kids at school went all day without food so I arranged with the cafe owner not far from one school to supply me. I got there early as she was making coffee for the beach boys and put my order in for sixty chapatis, and paid one of the lads to help me carry them down to the school. We waited for break-time, and as they came out, we gave them one each, including the teachers. I did this for the next three mornings. It was heartbreaking to see these kids so hungry, and rewarding to see their eyes light up as we handed out a simple piece of bread.

We got invited into the classroom every morning, and on the third day the class sang me a traditional Kenyan song as way of saying thank you. I got a tour of the school and it was then that I wondered where all these donated biros and writing books were, the kids certainly didn't have them. They were sharing bits of broken pencil and I picked up a book, felt it and it was made with the cheapest, roughest paper.

I knew I couldn't solve the problem. Corruption is, as I was discovering, more and more part of everyday life in Kenya, but the fact I was in control of my actions that day reassured me because I made sure those kids got their chapatis and no one else profited at my expense.

In the late-nineties most hotels were either half or full board, there weren't a lot of all inclusive deals back then so people would wander around looking for places to drink.

One place in particular was on Bamburi Beach; it was a big place and very cheap so it was always busy. One day I was there, thirty or forty American sailors walked in. Their ship had just docked in Mombasa for a few days. They stood in a group, looking at the bar, deciding what to get when a local kid of about ten starts putting on a show for them, doing backflips and juggling. At the end, the sailors did a collection for him.

After a few hours' drinking, the sailors start to get rowdy, laughing at each other's stories. I decided to take a walk outside. As I did, a little boy carrying eggs was in a hurry and was heading into the bar and to these American sailors.

"What you got there, son?"

"Eggs. Do you want to buy one?"

"How much?"

"Five bob?"

I picked one up, tossing it in my hand. "Look son, I know it's hot in Kenya but chickens can't lay eggs this hard."

"No, no, my mum boils them and I sell them."

I reached into my pocket; the next minute he readjusted his grip ready for his first sale and dropped the lot onto the concrete ramp. We both bent down to pick up his broken eggs and he started to cry.

"Here, take that home to mum." I hand him a five hundred shilling note. His face lights up and he's off down the beach again.

The bar was getting too rowdy. Most of the sailors were pissed; some of them had a job standing up so I stood outside and got talking to an older bloke. I wasn't sure of his rank but I guessed by his uniform he was in charge and the fact he was fairly sober. He was asking me questions about the area and he told me the ship was in the city for three nights.

As we talked I was distracted by a gang of girls who were on the beach calling the sailors, beckoning them to come out of the bar.

Whenever foreign ships came into Mombasa, everyone knew about it and it was a chance to make some money, including the girls who read the papers and followed the sailors everywhere.

A few of the drunk ones had left the main group, encouraging the rest to do the same and were making their way through the tables and chairs to see the girls. "Hitari Sana," I casually nodded to the girls.

"Pardon?" said the officer.

"Danger," I said. Those girls with your lads in that state. I explained to him what these girls are capable of and that was enough to order them all back into the bar. These drunken sailors were easy prey for the girls who would rob and fight to survive.

13. Loitoktok

Now it was time to turn my attention to my drugs. I needed to make new contacts get someone to supply me with drugs, some-one I could trust and that definitely ruled out using Del Boy and Rodders again.

I decided I was getting too familiar with Mombasa. My walka-bouts not only made me a target but it wouldn't take too long for word to get around, especially from the Mombasa-based beach boys who trawled the south coast beaches.

It was in Mombasa that I made a new friend. Tom, as he called himself, lived with his family in a town called Loitoktok and visited Mombasa once a week. I sat drinking and smoking outside a cafe on a quiet backstreet. Like with most situations, I didn't need to speak. An old white guy on his own in the city was enough for people to be curious. Complete strangers would just come up to me but I always needed to vet them. Most were just asking questions, some begged for money and anyone approaching me with the slightest mental affliction I gave a wide birth. The first thing I sussed out about Tom was his smart appearance. By Kenyan standards he had money and by the English words he used, I could tell he was well-educated. He liked to talk about his land and I didn't know what to make of him at first but then I realised he was just proud, showing off. He got income from tenants who rented the houses he owned. This is my man, I thought, and he lived in a place which was soon to become my favourite place in Kenya.

Loitoktok sits on the slopes of Kilimanjaro and its three vol-canic snow-capped cones dominate the natural park around for miles. It's one view I never got tired of. The town of Loitoktok is on the southeast side of the country and shares the border with Tanzania. It's roughly five thousand feet above sea level and the climate is a comfortable mid-twenties centigrade by day and mid-teens by night but the place is famous for dust – the dust is everywhere right up until rainy season.

We arrived after seven odd hours of bumpy road.

He owned about five acres of planted maize and was desperate for me to see it. "It's not far, we can walk," he said.

Two hours went by and we're still marching along, with him two strides ahead of me all the time. He tried to reassure me like a parent, "Not far now, nearly there."

I was soaked through and I felt my neck and face begin to burn. "You said that an hour ago." He smiled, swinging his arms backwards and forwards. This bloke never gets fucking tired.

We must have dropped down about two thousand feet.

I stopped. "That's it, game over. Not going any further. See that tree?" I nodded to it. "Well that's where I'll be, sitting under it, ok?"

He told me his mate lived nearby and would bring some drinks back later.

"Good idea. No rush, ok?"

The Acacia tree was the only tree around and the top spread out like an umbrella. I felt like I was on a David Attenborough film set. I slumped down against the tree, scanning the open space and tracing the route we'd taken. It was both stunning and surreal. I felt like I was in a picture with KMJ looking down over the setting. I stared, eyelids dropping into the hazy heat rising from the ground and the next minute I was asleep. I dozed, not sure how long for but when I opened my eyes again it didn't register straight away what I was actually looking at, but when I did, I froze.

A huge foot to my right. I looked up from the foot and my gaze followed a very long leg, right up to its body.

A giraffe.

85

It slowly folded its leg, adjusting position and for something so big it was incredibly graceful. Rooted to the spot I watched as it moved these massive feet a little at a time around the tree.

I slowly backed my self up against the tree to a standing position and moved carefully away to get a better look. This beautifully elegant animal had stood over me while I slept and was munching on the top leaves of the tree.

By the time Tom came back the giraffe had gone. "You must have been dreaming. No giraffes here," he said. "Never."

I know I dozed off but I am one hundred per cent sure that I didn't dream about that giraffe. It was weird, just me and this giraffe, sharing the same tree. That was a special moment.

We carried on walking and all I talked about was that giraffe but he wouldn't have it. No giraffes here, he kept telling me. "I have lived here all my life and I have never seen a giraffe around this area."

Hearing that made the experience even more special.

We finally got there. "There is my land," he said, pointing. All I could see was open quarry, not much soil, just stones everywhere. "I can grow maize here but the stones are a problem. I need to get the girls here."

The girls came from across the border in Tanzania.

We climbed a steep ridge and stood together. "See them? Look, you see them in the distance?" I could just make out spots moving in the distance on the Tanzanian side. They were working the land. "They travel around, clearing stones. They come here and work for me about six in the morning and work till one in the afternoon, take shade and go back home."

I asked him how much he paid them.

"Fifty, sixty bob a day" (sixty pence a day).

We walked back and cut through a field of long thick wild grass and all these butterflies started to rise from the ground all around me…thousands of them. The thick blanket of butterflies made me jump. I've never seen so many before.

"The rainy season must be near," he said.

He told me that at certain times of the year cars have to slow down and put their wipers on as they enter thick clouds of butter-flies.

14. The Stone Girls

It was getting late now and I realised I didn't have a place to stay. The nearest hotel was at the bottom of a coffee plantation which was very popular with tourists and charged twenty pounds a night. It was there I was thinking of staying until Tom offered to put me up.

"If you want, you can come and stay with me and my family for a few days," he said.

No money was mentioned but I was curious. "Ok, what d'you want in return? I'm not bloody picking up those stones!"

"No no, it's ok. When we go out you can buy me a drink and maybe some food now and again." That seemed like a good deal.

I met his mother and sister and a young girl who was the kitchen maid; she slept on the floor in the kitchen and was paid two thousand shillings (twenty pounds) per month.

I liked his mum and could tell the way Tom and his sister interacted with her that she was the boss of the family, the backbone. The land he was so keen to show me actually belonged to his mother and the longer I stayed with them the more I realised how much they depended on her. They didn't bother working, they didn't need to, and apart from collecting rent, he didn't do much else but get drunk.

That first night we all had supper together and he took me for another walk, this time a short one to see his other venture. The sign above the door said 'hotel' but it was more like a cafe with a room at the back and he charged six people to squeeze into it for the night.

The next day he wanted us to go back to see his land.

"I've seen it, remember?" doing my best to change his mind. "It took us two fucking hours and nearly crucified me, remember that?"

He laughed, patting my back to reassure me. "We'll take my car, but it's not a good road. It's easier to walk."

"It's fucking not, where's this car?"

We drove slow – his suspension was too low for this journey and his brother had the truck so it took us a while to get there, not the most comfortable of rides. The bumpy route shook me around a bit but it was better than walking. I wondered if his suspension would still be working for the way back. The crowd of women collecting stones had moved and were now on his land, spread around and bent over low to the ground, hands moving fast, whipping up stones and emptying each handful into a nearby bin.

"They don't see many mzungu out here and they may expect you to give something but don't, don't give them anything. You give to one the others will be jealous and fight." I didn't have much on me anyway but I felt the strongest urge to help at least someone, but I knew I would have to be discreet about it.

He summoned a few over in Swahili and told them I would like to chat to them.

They giggled, whispered and just stared at this old mzungu. I spoke Swahili which they understood, one woman in particular spoke very good English and I was already thinking ahead.

She told me about her family; three children and husband in Tanzania and was asking me all about England. I walked with her, chatting and picking up, throwing the odd stone.

I fished around in my pocket for the shilling note I knew I had with me and casually looked for the right size stone and in the secrecy of my pocket I began to wrap the stone up with the money making it as small as I could, rubbing and camouflaging it in dirt. I kept it closed in my hand and carried on throwing stones about with the other one. Now well away from the others I said goodbye, and walking away, I turned and threw my special stone, which landed at her feet. Surprised by my aim, she looked at this stone.

"Come on, back to work, pick it up."

She did, realising what it was, smiled and waved back at me.

We got back later and he wanted to take me for a drink. It didn't take me long to find out that Tom liked a drink.

I never used to drink much over there mainly because I needed my wits about me. I realised that a white, older man around these parts was an easy target but I did feel safer here than I did in the city.

The pub was only half-full but I've never been to a place like it; where everybody was at the same level of drunkenness. Everyone was pissed out of their heads. People swayed and staggered around the place, uneasy on their feet, bumping into things and shouting, laughing with each other.

"Thanks Tom, you take me to all the classy places."

"Hey, how can they afford to drink this much?"

"Changaa," he said.

He knocked the bar with his fist. "Mr Johnson would like to try a Changaa." A few gathered to watch the mzungu take his first Changaa.

"The best thing to do is knock it back – if you don't, it will burn," the barman said.

I wasn't looking forward to it but I couldn't let my audience down. As much as I tried to control my facial movements afterwards, I couldn't. My twisted grimace made everyone laugh and I gripped my neck with my hand, squeezing it trying to stop the burning hot lava scorching my throat. I had about three or four and they expected me to fall over.

Tom was impressed. "At least you can take your drink."

"I ain't taking anymore, of that I assure you." And I didn't.

Changaa is the local moonshine and it's the closest thing they have to whisky but it's much stronger and lethal, it's not even fermented properly. Seventeen people died in a Nairobi slum in 2010 because of a similar homemade brew, which they distil in their homes. If it doesn't kill it can blind you and causes a complete loss of control. It's lethal, very cheap to make and unpredictably dangerous.

I spent most of my time in Loi as his chaperone but, unlike him, I stayed away from the Changaa. I got the feeling he enjoyed having me around and would introduce me to everyone as his best friend. It was in a pub when he was quite drunk that I mentioned drugs.

"No problem," he said. "What do you want?"

"Resin, you know the resin blocks? Solid resin." Resin, I found out, is normally brought into the country from India and it's hard to get hold of as it goes mainly to the bigger cities.

I didn't mention it the next day but he remembered our conversation. We had lunch, I paid the bill and then he surprised me.

"Come on, let's get you fixed."

He introduced me to a bloke who was prepared to travel on his push bike to the next village to get it. "How far's that?" I said.

"Eight miles."

"On a push bike? And eight miles back?"

"Yeh, no problem."

"What does he get?"

"Fifty pence."

"FIFTY PENCE?" I couldn't believe the work involved for fifty pence.

Three days later the same bloke came back on his bike with a hundred fat cigar-sized cigarettes stuffed with grass in a bag – not what I had in mind but it was a start.

One cigarette cost me about eight pence, very cheap but I knew this wouldn't work, trying to sell tailored fags back home. So I unrolled each one, squashing the lot together and mummified it in cling wrap. Job done. I made sure the bloke on the bike made more than fifty pence for his trouble. I only brought this stuff back once – it was the smell, it was far stronger than anything else I'd done. Too risky, so I didn't use the man on his push-bike again.

15. Mule Man

I needed to make a new contact and my next was a risky one. Tom wanted to pay some cash into the bank so I went with him. I stayed outside and lit a fag and waited for him on the big steps outside the bank.

"Alright Mr Johnson?"

I turned to the voice. It was an askari (a soldier) who was guarding the bank. "How d'you know my name?"

"I have your description." This sounded serious. "Five foot eleven. Early sixties. Broad build and, seeing as you're the only white man around here, it must be you."

"Fifty-seven." He didn't answer. "My age, I'm fifty-seven." He apologised and smiled. "My life's been a hard one."

"You want some hard stuff?"

"No, no, I said hard life, I've had a hard life; it's a saying."

"Yes I know, but do you want some hard stuff? I can get it?" he said enthusiastically.

"What is this? Some sort of bloody set up? You tell the airport and you get paid twice, eh? Very good business. Very clever."

"No, I am genuine."

I looked at him trying to believe what he was saying. "What d'you mean, hard stuff?"

"Coke, heroin."

"Cannabis, but resin, you can get resin?"

"Yes, I can get it all." I listened to his hard sell.

"You give me one week, that's all I need. Yeh?"

"How much?"

"A hundred pounds sterling for one kilo. You know where you went for that meal the other day when you ordered a kilo of mbuzi (goat), well I was there. I watched you." The bugger had been following me.

"I'm there next Saturday at seven when it's busy. If I see you there at the same time I'll know you're interested, ok? I will have a kilo with me."

I told Tom what I was going to do.

"You are fucking crazy! You make a drugs deal with an askari? That bloke is a nightmare, everyone fears him. You can't be serious."

"He seemed to know all about me though."

"Well, I hope you've got this one right."

Yep I know, this one seemed a bit crazy but my instinct told me that if this was a set up to catch me out, then the money would have been lower, it wouldn't have mattered, the lower the amount the more attractive the deal and more chance of me taking the bait and snaring me.

The fact he asked for so much – four months' wages over there – confirmed it was for him and not a set up. So I went with it based on the fact that this was a poorly paid soldier in a third world country looking to make a bit for himself.

The following Saturday I made sure we got there early and took a table where I could watch the door. An askari came in and I panicked at first. I couldn't actually remember what he looked like. He could have been any soldier but to make sure I did see him he chose something heavy to drop on the floor. The noise made everyone look over to his direction and he looked straight at me. That was a signal, good enough for me. He made his way over and I was ready at this point. I got Tom to shift over a fraction so I could place my hand down on the bench and when he was near enough to me I opened and closed my fingers, flashing a glimpse of the money to him. As I did, he dropped something else on the floor next to my leg, picked it up, and reaching out, he put a plastic bag to the side of me. As he did, I moved my hand away and he took my money, didn't say a word and left the restaurant.

"You haven't got a chance to test that have you?" Tom said, referring to the quality.

"No, but I trust him." I don't think there's too many customers like me around. He rips me off and that'll be the end of a rematch." It turned out it was good stuff and I sold it in the UK for more than the grass.

It didn't take Tom too long to understand me and my humour, and my love of eccentric people. Tom was much more fun sober. Drink changed him to a demon.

"I need you to meet someone." And that's all he told me.

"Ooh, I like surprises," I said.

He took me to the other side of town to a bar, which at that time of day was empty; it was also dark and dingy.

"I was hoping to see the Mule Man here," Tom said to the barman.

The short fat bloke with half of one ear missing served us and told us he didn't live far but he didn't like visitors and it would be best to wait for him here as he normally came in for a drink at the same time every day.

We sat and waited for about an hour and were just about to leave when in he came. The door opened, blazing sunlight poured in and around his lanky silhouette, making him look holier than thou, like he was sent from heaven. He stood stooped over in the doorway, wearing his tatty straw hat taking it all in.

"Here he is, here he is." Tom livened up and waved him over. "Hello Mule Man, I'd like you to meet Mr Johnson."

He didn't say much, in fact Tom was doing all the talking.

"What do you want to drink then?" I said, rubbing my hands together.

"I'll have a whisky," he said, then he disappeared to the toilet.

"Hey, don't buy him anymore whisky."

"Why not?"

"Just watch when he comes back."

A large whisky was waiting on his return, and in Kenya, a large one means a tumbler of any large size full to the brim. He came back over and knocked the drink back in one, and looked at us both, waiting for the next one.

"Right, enough of that, Mr Johnson wants to see your shamba."

"My mule, you want to see my mule? You want to see it?"

"Yeh, we know all about your mule, come on, let's go."

We left the pub and turned off for about half a mile and followed a lane. "Look this," he said pointing. "My shamba." We looked out onto this empty field surrounded by woods but I couldn't see his house. As we got closer I could just make out his place through the trees. We walked around the back and he disappeared. We stood there waiting. He had bananas growing on the left of the gate and Sukuma Wiki or kale on the other side, but the majority of it was Banga (cannabis).

He reappeared, holding the rope of his mule, which I could see instantly had trouble standing. Its legs looked fragile, like they would collapse at any moment.

"He looks a bit sick to me," I said.

"Noooooo, he's always like that," said Mule Man. He yanked, pulling the rope tight and the poor thing wobbled towards us. Then I got it. I turned to Tom who was already smirking and shaking. This mule of his clearly had a penchant for cannabis.

I needed to say something now, a distraction to stop me from laughing out loud because I didn't want to offend Mule Man, who looked very intense, explaining in detail about his mule.

"A fine donkey you've got there, what's his name?" The end few words sounded a bit shaky as I did my best to hold it together.

"Carer." The name registered straight away and got louder in my head. Carer...CARER...a donkey out of his skull on drugs called Carer. He couldn't care less. He's fucking smashed.

My own private joke tipped me over the edge and I glanced quickly at Tom who refused to look at me but I could see his shoulders shaking. This mad lanky bloke in his straw hat with his stoned up donkey was all too much. Quick Terry, I need a question.

"How long will he last in this state?" was the only thing I could think of.

He didn't reply but Tom squealed back at me, "Oh not long, that's his third one this year."

"What's wrong?" said Mule Man, now a bit concerned. I bent down holding my sides, which started to ache, hiding and smearing away the tears rolling down my cheeks. No sound came out and Mule Man was still oblivious to the situation, asking me if I was alright.

The Mule Man and stoner of a donkey, god bless 'em, still makes me laugh now.

16. Leaving Do

My adventure in Loitoktok continued the following week with a wedding.

Tom was invited so he took me along as his plus one, and this was my first Kenyan wedding so I was looking forward to it.

The evening do was held in a large marquee, and judging by the guests, they had a bit of money. I found out it was customary at a Kenyan wedding to give the couple money and this guy with a microphone would announce names who came forward to drop their money in his basket.

Tom warned that as a mzungu I would be expected to give generously and that it wouldn't be a problem. The MC didn't bother with formalities of my name he just shouted 'mzungu' and everyone clapped and cheered, and as the only white face there, it had to be me.

"Hello mzungu...how much?" I showed him my note. "Two thousand bob," (£20) he announced to everyone who cheered again and then it went dark, pitch-black darkness. The generator took a few minutes to come back on by which time I was safely back in my seat, still holding my note and the MC carried on with the roll call and the rest of the donations. I told Tom about my cheap round and showed him the money. He just laughed. "Eh that's a bit embarrassing, we've got to visit them."

It was custom for the wedded couple to hold an open house for the next couple of days when wedding guests drop by and share tea with the married couple as a way of thanking them for their donation. I didn't feel too bad though because I wanted to keep my money back for the people who needed it.

Now wherever I went in the village I always seemed to see the same bloke; he stood out a bit because he was Indian, wore a suit and carried the same battered brown case around with him. I was guessing he sold something. About a hundred thousand Asians live in Kenya, mostly in and around Nairobi.

They were brought over by British India in the late 1800s to work on the Ugandan Railway and they were allowed to settle in East Africa when the work was completed. I met a few who formed the management team in the hotels I stayed in during my time there. "Yeh, I'm not sure what he sells but I've heard it's expensive," Tom said.

One day I went with Tom collecting rent, and while most of his tenants brought it to his house, he had a few who struggled with this arrangement so he did house visits.

I sat with him in one of his places, waiting with a woman for her husband to come back so he could pay us. I heard his Indian voice the other side of the door.

"Hodi?" (Can I come in?).

"Karibu," (Come on in, you're welcome) she said. The Indian salesman let himself in carrying blankets – handmade, good quality ones. I wondered why he bothered as we were here collecting money from people who could barely scrape together the rent, so I asked him.

"No, I thought they sold some grain. I thought they had some money." This guy would time his visits when the fields were harvested or planted, that's when people had money but today he was out of luck.

"No, they've got no money, I'm still waiting for the rent," Tom told him.

He grabbed his blankets and headed for the door.

"How much?"

"Six pounds," he said without hesitation.

"Ok, I'll take one." I paid him and handed the blanket to the woman. "That's for you."

"Thank you. Thank you very much," she said.

"I wish I'd never bloody come here now, I only came with him to collect the rent, it's just cost me six quid." We all laughed.

The husband came home and paid up and I asked Tom how much rent he'd collected.

"Ten pounds," he said.

"Ten quid for a week's rent and I've paid six quid for a blanket."

"Come on, let's get a beer."

A few days later, we were sat in someone else's house, doing the same thing, waiting for rent. A knock at the door was followed by a voice, "Hodi."

I looked at Tom. "It's not the same bloke, is it?"

"Karibu," she said, and in he came.

"Are you following us? You are, aren't you?" He shook his head denying it, but I wasn't sure.

"Look, you can't keep coming here at the same time as us, these people need to pay their rent not buy your bloody blankets." As he turned to leave, I handed him another six quid. "Come on then, let's have another blanket." I handed it to the very pleased looking lady of the house. One week or so later it happened again. We even looked around suspiciously for this little Indian fellow before stepping into the house. We were there about an hour this time sat drinking tea with the lady of the house. As soon as we heard the knock, we knew.

"Hodi." Unbelievable.

This time I shouted "Karibu" and it was him again. It was now clear he was scamming me; there was no way this was a fluke. Not for the third time.

"Yes, come in!" I shouted. Before seeing his face I held out money for him. In he came. "There's three bob there, I want a discount." Tom sat there in fits of laughter.

A few days turned into a few months and I was going to stay longer until he mentioned the rainy season.

I didn't want to leave the place. Loitoktok had found a place in my heart where I could have easily spent the rest of life, but it was time for work. I had three kilos to take back.

I told Tom when I was going and on the last day he organised my leaving do and told me his mate would pick me up. That afternoon at three a black Range Rover pulled up, a bloke got out and knocked on the door.

"Mr Johnson?"

"Yep."

"Come on, let's go."

"Where we off to then?" but he wouldn't tell me.

We drove a hundred yards or so, slowed up then stopped. The doors opened and three girls got in the back and were all over me in seconds and we drove off again. "What's all this then?" I shouted at the driver, trying to fight these girls off.

"It's all been organised by your mate."

"No way, I'm not staying in here with these sex maniacs. I'm not ready to die, just yet." He stopped the car, rolling my window down to where Tom was standing.

"You've met my family then."

He introduced me to his relatives who'd been groping me in the car and we parked up and went inside his sister's house, where they all surprised me.

People I'd met during my stay, including Mule Man and his stoned donkey, turned up to say goodbye. A spread of food waited for me on the table with booze laid on. I recognised the stone girls, the same twelve that spoke to me that day including the girl I threw money at who stepped forward with her present for me – a chocolate cake. Tom's driver walked in carrying a box – my present from Tom.

When I first met Tom we talked about wildlife and I told him one of my favourites was the Secretary bird, and would love to see one up close. It's different from most birds, maybe that's why I like it. It spends a lot of time on the ground foraging for food. The lower part of its legs are protected with armour-like scales, giving it protection against snakes and it's got big strong claw feet which it uses to hammer its prey to death. "This is for you, mzungu," Tom said, smiling proudly while handing it to me.

I peeked into the box and there it was. A Secretary bird. "We found it by the side of the road," he said, puffing his chest out, looking really pleased with himself. I know I wanted to see one up close but not an injured one in a box – a nice gesture though. I said my goodbyes and Tom drove me to Nairobi. I was going to miss Loitoktok.

The moment I stepped into the airport a big African woman jumped out from nowhere.

"What's in your case?" she barked.

"Dusty clothes." My quick, specific reply aroused more interest.

"Dusty clothes?" she questioned.

"Yeh, I've been to Loitoktok, all my clothes need a good wash now, it's a very dusty place."

"I know, my sister used to live there."

We chatted on and she became my friend and eventually left me to check in and board the plane. All airport staff have different methods of detection; hers was to scare the shit out of people but I was ready as usual.

17. Masai, and a London Black Cab

I went back to Loi a few more times over the next two years but the only problem with the seven and half-hour journey was the road.

In 2010, the President opened the newly refurbished main road near Loi. The C109 links Mombasa to Nairobi and the government project started in 2007, transformed 300km of road with smooth bitumen, complete with drainage and also included part of the road into the town. When I used it the road was at its worst, bumps, lumps and holes everywhere.

A few hours of main road, then it changes as you take a turn towards the mountains and the road gets worse. One of the drivers in Mombasa had a relative who could take me. I just had to find him first. I roamed the back streets and could see the locals looking at me, wondering what this old white guy was up to. It didn't take him long to find me and he asked me if I'd buy him a drink at a nearby hotel and we sat and chatted.

I told him I had to meet someone in Loitoktok and needed to go. He drank up and told me to wait. Ten minutes later, a shabby, decayed-looking bus full of rust pulled up near where I sat. He parked up and jumped down, walking towards me, leaving the thing rattling, vibrating on the spot behind him.

"You can't be serious." I said, chuckling. I got a closer view, peering into one of the dusty windows – it was a right state. It seated about thirty but most of the seats were missing and was crammed with all sorts of shit, even had loose chickens flapping around inside from open cages.

"It's ok, you can sit in front with me," he said, as if everything was going to be alright. I heard voices and noises as they shuffled around. "Quick! Mzungu coming." His family were crouching down, trying to hide from me. It was clear from this that this bus was his home. We set off and our first stop was a petrol station.

"Right Mr Johnson, would you like a drink or anything, this is the last stop. No more shops, ok?"

He came back and handed me a bottle of squash and I noticed a bag in his other hand which he fiddled with, unscrewing the cap.

"Whisky?" I said. He offered me the bottle.

A seven-hour journey on a bus which was ready to fall apart at any moment, and now the driver starts swigging whisky.

"Yeh, I always drive better when I've had a drink."

This was me taking a risk again but I got the feeling this wasn't his first drink driving offence and this jalopy I was on with his family was his home so I found myself believing his claim of being a better driver under the influence. Not a normal thing to rationalise but this wasn't a normal place. He took a few more swigs and we set off again.

Twenty minutes in and we saw police cars parked, splayed across the road forming a road block. They stood waving us to stop.

His relaxed mood changed and he was now cursing aloud in Swahili, words I've never heard before, then for my benefit in English. "Bastards! They normally come and get on my bus; they won't today because I have a mzungu with me."

Three policeman all with AK47s stood alongside the bus. One waved the end of his gun, beckoning the driver to him. He jumped down, taking his whisky with him, taking big serious strides and he gave 'em hell.

"You bastards," he said. "I've already given you five hundred today.

What more do you want?"

I stayed seated, watching as he gave three armed policemen a hard time, his arms moving wildly in the air, still clutching his whisky. In the end he seemed to run out of energy and stood quite calm and then he eventually paid up and climbed up back behind the wheel again and explained.

"What just happened is a problem. The Police abuse their power and take money off everyone on the road. To drive in Kenya you have to keep money back for these situations, if you don't they can take what they want from you and if they take my bus then I am finished."

"Even if I didn't drink whisky they would still stop me and make me pay so that's why I carry on drinking. Fuck them."

After a while we came off the main road and were now bumping around on a dirt track. The landscape looked the same for miles around and with every approaching hill I thought we were there, but every time we reached one hill we carried up over to the next one – the scenery was never ending. Seven hours went by very slowly.

I noticed the bottle he swigged from was now half full and the road was getting worse and he kept jerking the wheel, swerving to avoid the potholes.

"You know that lorry that just passed us on the opposite side?"

"Yeh."

"I reckon he's just killed a lame or sick animal, maybe a zebra."

"How the hell do you know that?"

"Look up there," he said.

In the distance vultures hung in the air.

"They've spotted meat," he wagged his finger. Even though he was drinking he was talking quite sensibly and navigating the bus like an expert.

"Keep your eyes out for the Masai looking for their dinner."

We went up and over another hill and with what looked miles of road ahead there were, as he said, three Masai warriors walking at the side of the road. We passed them and a little further along was the dead Zebra they were looking for by the side of the road. I was impressed. He was bang on with his prediction.

The next time I went to Loi, I landed at Mombasa and went through security into arrivals; there was a bloke there, waving around a picture of me. He lowered himself under the barrier and walked beside me, explaining Tom had sent him.

Nice surprise I thought, but when I saw this bloke's car I changed my mind, went back into the airport and ordered a coffee. Knowing how rough the journey to Loi was, this guy was out of his mind if he thought I was getting in his car. It was a wreck, the suspension was fucked before we even started; rusted with windows missing – he must pay the police a lot to keep this on the road. "No, it's fine," he said. "Look," and he turned the ignition over and, perfect timing, black smoke pumped out the back. Thanks, but no thanks.

Another driver from the airport meet and greet came over to my table and had watched me and this bloke, outside with his rust bucket. His company left it too late to cancel a job so he was wasting his time at the airport but overheard me talking. He showed me his car. "Just like home, eh?" We both looked at his gleaming black London cab. A black London taxicab waiting for me in Africa; that was fate.

He'd never been to Loitoktok; I think he was expecting a local fare. "I need to go tonight at midnight."

"Too dangerous at night," he said.

"Ok, I'll speak to someone else then I have to get there for the morning."

"No, wait, please give me an hour; I need to ask someone first." I could see he didn't want to give the job up so I agreed. Less than half an hour he was back with his mate.

"He will come with us just in case." Just in case of what? Now I started to worry. We got to the dusty uneven part of the journey and I could hear the guys panic at the noises the car made as the bottom of it hit the bumpy road. The other guy was his business partner and owned a fifty percent share of the car – I could see it was their pride and joy. Not many black London cabs around these parts. It was pitch black and I sat bumping around in the back until he eased off the speed and the car trickled to a stop. Out of fuel was my first reaction but then I could feel the jerky movements of the car, and winding down the window, I could hear the shredded tyre.

We can fix this, a bit dark but it's ok. They didn't share my confidence and by their faces they looked worried. I followed them both out of the car.

I could hardly make out where they were standing it was so dark but from their chit-chat they were standing at the back.

We got tools out of the back and set about changing the wheel. "This is not the place to get a puncture," he said as he pushed down on the wrench to get each wheel nut off.

"Bandits use this road at night." That's why he wanted his mate with him – back up.

We'd all but finished when we all looked up and saw spots of light on the horizon beaming towards us.

"Quick! We need to go!" Now these two really panicked. "We need to get the car off the road." I stood bent over the back, arms outstretched in a pushing position waiting for the other two who were arguing about the tools that we left lying around, then they spoke in Swahili blaming each other for taking the fare in the first place. This car was going some, the lights were getting bigger and were closing in fast. Keeping our lights off while we struggled in the dark was now looking like a good idea as we pushed the car into the bushes and waited, watching the lights close in and rush past us.

We could now all breath again. It may not have been bandits but on this road at night you didn't take that chance.

When we got near I gave him directions from memory. "When we get to the top of the hill you need to take a right and you'll see a concrete building and that's the morgue."

He asked me where I needed to meet my mate. I hadn't got a clue but it wouldn't take too long to find me, there couldn't be many like me around, they both laughed.

We parked up and smelt food cooking and realised how hungry we all were so we sat outside at the nearest place and I called this guy over from his open kitchen and ordered a kilo of goat and a pot of rice to share. They both looked around the place and told me how shocked they were. These two blokes were from poor backgrounds but they had jobs which gave them food to feed their family and a home to live in. This little part of town we overlooked was about as poor as you could get. Children sat in and around raw sewage and rubbish that spewed out from a hole and flowed like a river between ramshackle buildings that looked like they were ready to collapse and fold at any time.

My contact turned up; it was another mate of Tom's who was away in Tanzania on business, that's what he told me anyway. Tom briefed him on my appearance and where to find me. There was a problem. Banana Man would be supplying me, but not in bananas, and it wouldn't be until the morning. I had to break it to both drivers about the unexpected overnight stay. The plan was to do the trip in a day but they didn't seem to mind. I told them I would pick up the tab for the stay and pay them extra for their time so it was all good.

Money was tight so I chose the cheapest place for us to stay. It was a rundown place, and if it hadn't had the word 'Hotel' outside, you would be none the wiser; in fact, it wasn't much different from all the other slum shacks around. Well, what do you expect for a hundred bob a night. We all stayed in separate rooms; mine had a flimsy lock on the door, so I moved a wardrobe in front of the door, and before I did I went and told the others to do the same.

The next day was market day; I told the drivers to wait at the hotel while I went to look for a man selling bananas. I thought it might be difficult in a large market but Tom's mate said they call him Banana Reggae Man because he always plays reggae. Knowing my luck, I'll turn up and there'll be lots of stalls selling bananas and playing reggae. I found him, and lucky for me he was the one playing *One Love* by Bob Marley full blast. He greeted me like a long-lost brother, wrapped his arms around me and hugged me. I got two kilos of bananas for the journey back and two kilos of grass. The drivers were none the wiser and we made the trip back without a puncture this time.

18. The Real Thing

As I said before, I had become very good at smuggling drugs. I know luck helped me along the way but I had a talent for getting out of tight situations. The other side to being a successful drug smuggler is selling the stuff and I wasn't very good at that bit.

I could have been but all my energy and focus was more on the smuggling bit and when I got back to the UK I was just relieved it was all over – until the next time of course. I never questioned or challenged or haggled with people about costs, and at times knew I was being ripped off, but as long as I made enough to get by on then I was happy.

One bloke did change my way of thinking though. It was a mate of a bloke I worked with and he just came out with it one day. He had a private job for me; it was someone else's work that the customer wasn't happy with. He was told I specialised in patios and was good at them. He was keen for me to have a look at the job and a quote him to put it right. He picked me up and we went around the back of the house. "Not good is it?"

"Not good. Not good."

"Who the fuck did this? A demented gorilla?" We both stood and laughed at the sight. "They had a fucking earth tremor here or what?"

The large space was a choppy sea of concrete slabs which had sunk in the middle, about two hundred of them had literally been thrown together. It looked a complete mess. We walked over it and I took charge. "Right, all these need to come up," I said, waving my finger around, "and put against there." I pointed at his boundary wall.

"Ok."

"Then, I need five tonnes of sand and cement."

"Yep, yep, no problem. I'll get that for you."

It took me about a week to put things right and then he paid me. In fact he overpaid me, which I thought was odd, and counted the money out on his coffee table.

"You fancy a drink then?" I needed to go but decided to stay for one anyway; he was dropping me off so I couldn't say no.

"Got any Bacardi?"

"Er yeh, I think so should have some from Christmas."

He opened the cupboard and started rooting through it, moving, clinking bottles, trying to find the right one.

"Bacardi's like a dog, it's not just for Christmas," I shouted back at him.

"Got any Coke to go with it?"

"Nah, got lemonade," he shouted back.

"Yeh, that'll do."

He walked back in with two iced tumblers and handed me one.

"I need a kilo of coke." I nervously took a few short sips, trying to digest his words. "I'm serious, I need a kilo of coke."

"Ok, what's that got to do with me?"

"Well, I know you go to Kenya a lot, the boys told me you can get a bit of grass for them but I need coke."

"No." I shook my head as well, to make sure he understood. "No way, not doing that."

He changed the subject and we chatted for a bit about the bloke who ruined his garden but I could tell where the conversation was going again. "Why don't you risk it for something worthwhile?"

He dropped me back home but it was that question that changed my mind. Why was I risking my neck so often for so little? I was putting myself through it all, risking everything and getting ripped off at the end of it. It didn't make any sense to me. The more I thought of his offer the more I liked it. My holiday would be paid and I would stand to make twenty grand. Twenty thousand pounds. That sort of money would set me up for life in Kenya. I called him the next day.

We met up and he gave me a grand for the holiday, added a bit more for expenses and five grand in twenty pound notes to buy the coke.

"Remember, wet your finger, dab it and rub into your gum, if it tingles it's the real thing, if it doesn't then don't buy it." I had no idea about coke and the only reason I knew it was white because I'd seen Tubbs open a consignment of coke on *Miami Vice*. I'd never seen or tasted it before so I was a bit nervous about the whole situation.

"If it doesn't tingle, don't buy it."

I couldn't relax. I tried to enjoy myself on this particular trip but couldn't – my mind would always come back to the reason I was there. Coke. I was bringing back serious stuff, a class A drug, and what made it worse; the holiday seemed to fly by and the last two days loomed before my flight home so it was time to get to work.

Now, looking for a class A drug in a foreign country was a challenge. Grass was never a problem, most villagers grew it and smoked it.

I had a chat with one of the beach boys who offered to get me some but I didn't want to involve them – that would be asking for trouble. I made out it was for personal use and then changed my mind, telling him I'd stick with the grass. I did manage to get some information; he told me the dock area was the best place to go for it if you wanted to buy in bulk. The docks it was then.

I caught a Matatu to the docks and was met by the usual crowd, touting and begging as I got out.

"Can I help you?" said this lad who had gotten off the Matatu with me.

I answered him with the first thing that entered my head.

"No, I'm looking for my friend, he was here about an hour and a half ago," I said – anything just to get rid of him.

"A white man."

"Er yeh."

"Did he have a hat on?" I wasn't sure where this was going, I just answered looking around, to see where I could go to lose him. "I expect so."

"And glasses, was he a tall man?"

"Er yeh, anyway gotta go now."

"Have you got any money for me?"

"I haven't mate, I will have later on if I find you, ok?"

I went around the corner and chose a cafe to sit in while I thought out my next move.

"You want dope?" It was same bloody kid, I couldn't shake him off.

"No, no."

"Coke?" Even though I told him I wasn't interested, he'd read my reaction perfectly. "I know somebody can get coke for you."

"I don't want coke," I said, keeping up the pretence. It felt odd dealing with a kid for drugs.

"Do you know Johno from the beach?"

"No."

"Well, he knows you."

Maybe a friend of Del Boy and Rodders, I thought. "How d'you know me?"

"I've seen you before and you look for drugs."

This kid had been on my trail, gotten on the same bus and was desperate to make some money.

"Ok, where can I get this coke?"

"If I show you where, will you give me money?"

I agreed and followed him. This kid, like most ducker and divers, had a connection with the beach boys, and as much as I didn't want to deal direct with them I could tell they were somehow involved, but I didn't have any other choice. He only took me so far and then pointed to one of six or seven timber shacks along the docks.

I knocked and waited. No answer so I just pushed the door open and faced six blokes; only one spoke English, the others stood around, they were darker, I think they were Sudanese and I couldn't understand a word they were saying. The room had a veranda at the back and I could see kids playing. They all watched me as I spoke.

I told them what I needed, and two guys moved from the chest seat where they sat, one opened the hinged lid, rummaged through it picking up packages, guess weighing them in his hand, until he got the right one.

"That's a kilo." He slapped it on the table. I wasn't going to argue with him or ask him to weigh it properly, I just wanted to get out as soon as possible – the atmosphere was similar in Likoni when I gate-crashed those blokes counting money. In fairness, my estimate of a kilo is a bag of sugar, this was the same size and when I picked it up it felt like a kilo. Good enough for me. We stood around the package which he opened on the table. My mind suddenly flashed back home. 'Whatever you do, when you get it test the stuff, wet your finger, dip it and rub it on your gums – if it tingles and goes numb, no problem'.

They watched me and it did exactly that. Satisfied with my gums now electrified with tingles, I reached down and put my hand on the package.

"Right, I'm going to put this in my bag, who's coming back with me?"

"Back where?"

"Back to the hotel, you didn't think I'd carry that sort of money around with me, did you?"

"How much did you say?"

"Four and a half thousand English."

He picked the largest in size to accompany me back to the hotel and my first cocaine deal was sealed, just had to get the stuff to the UK now.

The last day of that trip I woke up and realised what I was about to do. A class A drug – cocaine, a kilo of cocaine, suddenly my sentence in a Kenyan prison had doubled.

First, to get through Mombasa then London Gatwick without being caught. As we approached the roundabout outside the airport, I could see soldiers with Alsatian dogs, as if they had been tipped off or something. The first trip feelings started to fester. My heart raced. The thing is, I'd never seen the dogs and soldiers at the airport before so it was natural to worry but then I rationalised it in my head as some sort of security measure that was now in place. Nothing to do with you Terry, carry on. I got off the bus, one of the boys as usual grabbed my bag for a shilling.

Nairobi airport is about sixteen miles from the town and not very big with a paved walkover for passengers. I was now getting used to seeing the ten years in prison notice, but today it flashed through my mind and stayed there – after all, I was smuggling a kilo of coke through this time.

It was my turn to put my case on to be x-rayed and just by luck a bloke came over and went to pick up my case and I smelt his breath. To anyone else it was just a stale odour but to me it was something else. I looked him in the eye and said, "Eh, you've been drinking Changaa." He now looked flustered, fidgety. Bingo. I knew I was right.

"You're drunk on duty, aren't you? You're fucking drunk, you've been drinking Changaa." I looked around to see who was listening and the two at the screen looked a bit shifty as well.

"And you two," now wagging my finger at them.

The guy picking up my case tried to hush me down with his finger to his mouth and my case went through without a problem and he hurried me away. Perfect.

My guess is these three fellas who work together probably socialise together and went to the same bar/party the night before. Even if they saw something suspect in my bag on the monitor I don't think then was the time to stop and question me. I knew this, they knew this, so I just picked my case up and sauntered through to passport control. Now I just had to get through Gatwick.

Waiting at the carousel for my case to appear, I looked across at the green 'Nothing to Declare' channel and a man in his forties stood in a back office doorway moving in and out of it, keeping an eye on us around the carousel and chatting with staff in the room. I looked over again and this time he had his back to me as he leant into the doorway propped by one shoulder with his feet crossed and was gently tapping the antenna of his walkie talkie into his cheek as he listened to the conversation. Every so often he would laugh, move away from the doorway look over to us and return to the doorway and carry on chatting. This, I thought, was a good sign – happy and distracted. I chose my moment, grabbed my case and followed a couple with noisy straggling kids behind them. The man had disappeared from his spot but as I got closer he reappeared, acknowledging the family first, smiling at the kids, then looked straight at me.

"What's in the case, young man?"

As soon as I heard the word 'young' I knew he had a sense of humour.

"Drugs, Sir."

"Okay, on ya go," and waved me through, enjoying the banter with a cheesy grin. Terry, you've done it again.

It was luck again I know, but I watched and judged this guy's mood before we spoke and rehearsed my answer ready for him. Any change in my mood would have given him a chance. He had a sense of humour and he appreciated mine.

19. The Switch

The day after I landed, I called Patio Man and he came to see me. I got in his car with a man in the back so big and wide I couldn't see the back window. I watched this guy as we filed into Patio Man's house; he had to adjust himself to get through the door, stooping down to get his over-sized shaven head in.

Patio Man was in a chirpy mood and went straight to the cupboard and got the Bacardi out and walked towards me with one hand behind his back, smiling. He swung it round and was holding a bottle of Coke to go with the Bacardi.

"See? I remembered." He lined three glasses of ice up on the table and poured the drinks.

"Now that's your Coke," he said, screwing the cap. Hint taken. They watched as I unzipped the rucksack, lifting the package out carefully like I was diffusing a bomb. I was holding a hundred grand so I understood how important this was to them. Holding a knife and without completely getting up, Patio Man moved, taking his chair with him to get closer to the table.

He reached for the package, slicing at it, tearing into the layers. His mate had moved and was now alongside him, his massive carved muscular back bent over, his nose almost touching the table. They both dabbed at the same time brushing their gums in unison. They both reacted differently, Patio Man raced dabbing again and starting to frown, looking a bit tense and the big guy sat back in his chair upright and was still brushing on his first dab, his eyes fixed to the fireplace.

"This is flour," Patio Man said slowly, looking at me and then to his mate. "Fucking Flour."

The big guy didn't budge, just sat there wide-eyed, nodding slowly in agreement as if he was day-dreaming. Patio Man turned to me. "This is fucking flour. This is flour," The more he said it the more I found myself unable to move, frozen to the spot.

"Look, taste it," I believed him and didn't move. He came towards me and got in my face. "Go on, fucking taste." He was waiting, watching my reaction as I tried it myself.

I rubbed it, hoping he was wrong but he wasn't. No Tingle. No feeling, just a starchy uncooked taste of pastry. Yep that was flour.

"What did I tell you? Mmm....? What did I fucking tell you?"

"I did. I did. I tasted it and it tingled, it more than tingled, it fucking vibrated my teeth. They've fucking switched it. This is not the stuff I tasted."

"That's fucking four and half grand," he said. "Gone."

I slumped back into my chair and told them about the six men in the hut down at the docks. The big guy kept quiet all the time and just listened I was expecting him to explode at any moment. He worked the doors at nightclubs and was due in court for sentencing and was expecting to go down for a year or two.

Patio Man asked him if he wanted in on the deal, and the money from selling the coke would see his family alright while he was inside. Knowing this about him I was preparing myself for the worst. He'd been ripped off and he was going down so he didn't have much to lose. But he surprised me.

He got up, dropped his shoulder down and dabbed it again, but this time just rubbed it on the end of his finger, staring at it, then lifted the package at one end turning it over, inspecting it and then looked up at me.

"I believe him."

He turned to Patio Man. "I believe his story."

"This package has been done by experts and he (now pointing at me) is no fucking expert."

"So fucking what! We've lost our fucking money." I sat quiet and listened to them argue. I felt a bit easier knowing that the big guy was on my side. It went quiet for a few minutes. "What we're going to do ... is send him back."

"Yep." I just nodded. Relieved to hear a solution. "That's it, I'll go back over."

I said it like it was so easy. I couldn't think of anything worse than to put myself through all that again. This was supposed to be my last time. If I didn't go these guys knew where Ann lived and I didn't want to involve her in my mess – that would be unfair. So I had no choice, but first I had to get some money together and find work, which I did in Shrewsbury.

I worked in a factory with Dave back in the early eighties and kept in touch now and again; he knew a lot of people and it was a place I knew quite well having worked near there a few years back.

I called him up but he was in Australia; his brother, who was house sitting, told me about jobs going at a local quarry. After speaking to his brother, Dave called me and told me about his sons who were sharing a flat that Dave owned and said he would arrange for me to stay with them for a few months, which was ideal. He said he would speak to them and let me know. I took his number and called him the next day and it was all arranged.

20. Crow Man

They were kids the last time I saw them and complete opposites. Lee was a prolific shoplifter and held the record for burgling his local shop three times in the same year. His own stupidity caught him the end. He got a taxi to wait outside the shop in the early hours, alarm wailing in the background he clambered onto the back seats with bin bags stuffed with fags and sweets. The police arrested him the same day after the driver gave a full description and where they could find him. If he hadn't fucked up and got caught there were plenty around ready to grass because he loved to brag about it all. He was into eighties action films like *Rambo* and *The Terminator* and would bunk off school to watch them over and over. Unlike his heroes he was bony thin but desperate to be noticed.

Once he was caught on the roof of Woolworths in Swindon trying to smash his way through the skylight.

Gavin turned out to be gay. No surprise to anyone who knew him growing up. He was very feminine as a boy and he felt more relaxed in the company of girls. He embraced the whole dressing up thing, which carried through to his late teens. He was at one stage so desperate to be a woman he was prepared to undergo a full sex change operation but he couldn't convince the doctors and counsellors, and lacked the necessary commitment and maturity needed before they would agree to the surgery. He just couldn't cope with living life as a woman for two years.

His childlike personality wasn't tough enough to deal with the day-to-day public stuff; the stares, whispers and the abuse that goes with the transgender thing. In the end, he just settled for life as a gay man. Unlike Lee, he was a good-looking kid, thick glossy meticulously styled hair and long eye-lashed hazel eyes. Never short of boyfriends he also had a few older married men on the go who he'd meet up with now and again to spoil him. He loved the attention, the gifts and the money.

He worked for agencies; mainly cleaning jobs, he loved Abba, *Star Wars*, and hairdressing. His chipped discoloured front tooth had to be removed because of his fizzy drink habit – two litres a day.

He left school with no qualifications but turned the love of his life into a job –hairdressing. It was more sweeping up, making coffees and washing than styling and cutting, but he didn't mind, he was happy just being there. He loved everything about working in a salon, the gossipy chit-chat and being surrounded by women all day. That was good enough for him.

Lee was a DJ – well he thought he was. He spent most of his time in amusement arcades, playing the slots with his dole money. One place had an under-eighteens disco on a Friday and he used to help 'set up' for the DJ. At first he just hung around waiting to be asked to fetch and carry speakers and decks from the back of his van until it became a regular thing and was eventually paid to assist the DJ. Of course he told the young girls at the disco that he was a proper DJ and was just helping his mate out.

When he wasn't sleeping or carrying disco equipment he was helping Lara Croft get to the next stage on his Play Station.

He met Kylie, a sixteen-year old A level student, at the club. She came from a big family who owned a tyre fitting company. It wasn't just the ten-year age gap that bothered Eric, her dad. When he met his daughter's first boyfriend, he stayed polite but deep down he felt let down and resented him. In his eyes, the bloke was a tosser – no good for his daughter and he felt helpless about the situation. When her parents found out she was pregnant with his kid they virtually disowned her and she ended up moving in with him.

Gavin was allowed to move in on the condition that he cleaned and cooked and took full advantage of his brothers OCD. He had three different cleaning jobs and was a bit of a grafter when it came to cleaning. Every socket in his room had a plug in air freshener and if that wasn't enough, he kept a can of Alpine Fresh with him at all times, handy for Lee's farts. His room was a shrine to George Lucas, he bought a second-hand cabinet from the small ads and filled it with *Star Wars* memorabilia; figures, space ships, playing cards, flags, posters and managed to keep every one dust free and shiny.

Their second floor flat was one of four converted from a shabby rundown Victorian house back in the eighties. The open plan living/kitchen area spanned the width of the house with two sash windows which overlooked the main road and two bedrooms off the same landing.

When I got there we agreed I'd stay in Gavin's room as I was the one paying rent and he would sleep on the sofa, he didn't mind that, after all, he loved night-time and would sit alone watching tv, getting stoned, drunk or both. He drank cider like he used to drink cola and smoked hash. Most nights he'd do this to oblivion but amazingly still manage to hold down his jobs.

Once I woke up in the night when I heard a crash downstairs. I stood on the landing looking down at a dark figure and turned the light on. It was Gavin, completely naked, steadying himself holding a tray with a skyscraper pile of jam sandwiches. He stood swaying, trying to put a foot on the bottom stair. I stood back into my doorway and watched him climb the stairs he passed me on the landing, not even realising I was there. Thinking he had got to the doorway he turned and slammed into the wall, his tray now flat against his chest. I could see how stoned he was by his slow motion reaction and concentration as he stepped back from the wall. Unfazed by it all, he used one hand to balance the tray and the other to collect together his mangled supper. The next day I was, as always, the first up, ready for work and opened the living room door and there he was. Naked. His ass in the air slumped over the tv, still fast asleep and the same jam sandwiches scattered all around him.

On another day, I dozed in the chair, waking up to shouting. I looked around but realised the sound was coming from outside. I ran to the window and saw a boozed up Gavin on the flat roof, he was near the edge, ranting. I pulled the sash window up and his voice boomed into the room. I tried to talk him down but he wasn't having any of it so I turned to his brother who ignored everything that was going on around us.

"Lee, your brother's on the roof, he's gonna fucking jump. Don't just sit there, come on!" No reaction, not a word, he just sat there clicking, moving his controller, not taking his eyes off the game.

I shouted at him and this time he reacted, but slowly and with a lot of effort and a big sigh. "Yeh, I know." He stood up edging himself slowly away, still holding the controller and watching the screen. He stretched the lead, playing and talking to me at the same time, leant back and glanced quickly through the open window. "Get off the roof, Gavin," he said without emotion, and sat back down again.

"Lee!" I couldn't believe his reaction.

"He's done it before, he did it last year, he always does it. He won't jump. He gets depressed about stuff, his weight and that."

I found out that he couldn't stand the thought of getting older, had nightmares about dying and got depressed about his weight. So then how did he cope with those issues? He ate, smoked and drank himself into a stupor, which then made him want to go and jump off buildings.

Lee's prediction was right. Ten minutes later, Gavin got off the flat roof and dived for the fridge, grabbing his two-litre size bottle of cider and disappeared off to play his Abba music.

I spent three months waking up to Ewoks and Darth Vader but I did what I had come to do. Lee had just started working. They threatened his dole money would stop so he had to get a job. That was hard for him; he was naturally lazy and hated work, but he knew someone down the quarry. A few days later he got me an interview.

"Malcolm, this is Terry, my dad's mate I told you about."

Malcolm was site foreman and I knew exactly what he was

thinking and started with the questions. "What's your background, what have you done?"

"A bit of farm work, labouring, but mostly gardening and laying patios."

"You ever worked in a quarry before?"

"Nope."

I was fifty nine at the time and most of his crew were in their twenties and thirties.

"Ok, you start today and we'll see 'ow it goes, eh?" he said, forcing a smile, trying to be friendly, "but I'll warn you, this is fucking back-breaking work."

The quarry mined slate. Diggers would fill and lift giant buckets and empty them into mountains of slate for the public to come along and pick up. We had to sort them individually and separate them with a chisel and hammer and fill containers which were then lifted away by the diggers. It was exactly how he described it, but I needed to impress. The others would take the ten-minute walk back to the office for breaks and an hour for lunch, but I never stopped, I ate on the job and the only time I stopped was every so often for a moment or two to straighten my back. I liked it when they left me to it, just me and a load of crows in an open quarry. They showed up the moment it was quiet, knowing I would feed them. I used to break up bits of my sandwich, but one day I noticed one not eating with the rest; he'd pick up food instead and disappear to the other side of the bank. This intrigued me, so one day I followed this bird up and over the bank and found the crow with a stockpile of bread that he'd collected and was supplying the other crows. A Crow dealer, that made me chuckle. It was my fascination with these birds that got me the nickname of 'Crow Man'. Who is this nutter that doesn't take his breaks and talks to the crows? they used to say.

A nutter maybe, but by the end of the day my basket was bigger and stacked higher than anyone else's and all the talking and my hard graft got me noticed by the boss.

Lee and the others took their break and watched me work.

"Your dad's mate is a fucking machine, 'ow old is he?"

"Not sure, same as my old man. I think...sixty something."

"What's he doing living with you then?"

"Dunno really...me dad called me and said his mate needed a place to stay for a while..." he said, trying to talk through mouthfuls of bread.

I think they all expected me to ease up after that first day but I carried on at the same rate. The boss didn't say much but I knew he was happy and allowed me to drive a digger. Normally new starters proved themselves for a year or so before they were trusted to operate the diggers, mainly because the terrain was difficult and fragile and they were expensive to replace. If I was thirty I could have coped much better but the job left me completely knackered. I did the same thing at the end of each day. My body ached, throbbing with pain, so after eating quick from tins, I slumped into a chair at six and slept, and that's where I stayed until Gavin came crashing through the door.

My day at the asylum would start at about five-thirty. I didn't need an alarm call, Connor did that for me with the tv on its highest volume. Now three, Lee's kid was into everything and nearly always unsupervised.

One morning, I walked into the kitchen and found him standing in the sink, shaking a box of cornflakes. I guessed he'd been there a while because the floor was a sea of different coloured cereals. I also caught him trying to take a plug apart once. He was about to poke the socket with a knife when I came into the room.

Things turned from bad to worse for Lee; first he was sacked for his laziness. He used to fuck around throwing stones instead of working and the following week his girlfriend came to her senses, packed her stuff, took the baby and went home. The day I left, the boss called me into his office.

"Terry mate, I wish I had more like you here. Take my number, call me anytime if you want to come back, alright? So long as you can work like that, there'll always be a job here for you." He handed me an envelope and I said goodbye to the lads. It was £3000 plus £340 holiday pay, and seeing as I didn't have a proper contract, I wasn't really entitled to holiday pay so it was nice of him to do that.

21. One Last Trip

A week later, I flew back to Kenya.

I was back on track and had the money to do one last trip but it wasn't going to be coke. I didn't feel comfortable doing it last time and was dreading the prospect of doing it all over again. I was at the time only too happy to agree with Patio Man and the Hulk but that was more out of desperation. I was ready to agree anything that day, just to get my ass out of there.

I was going to bring back grass and with the sale of that and my savings from the quarry, my intention was just to pay them off the five grand I owed and forget the whole drug smuggling thing. Stepping up and taking a class A drug back through three airports frightened the shit out of me and by the law of averages there's only so much luck to go around. Up till then I'd more than my fair share.

I sent Sharon a letter saying I'd be flying back to Kenya and gave her my flight details and a time. I had presents for my boy and my plan was for us to stay in different hotels along the beaches.

Now that day, the day I left for Kenya didn't start well. My plane was delayed for seven hours and when I eventually landed I bumped into the landlord's neighbour from the village. He spotted me. I was tired, just about to get into a taxi when he shouted my name and bounded over, in the mood for talking. The last time I saw him was with my son and Sharon swimming on one of the local beaches. I told him I was heading to the village to see my son then he waffled on about his job; he worked in the city as a driver and was telling me all about his day. I did my best to listen but all I wanted to do was to get going.

It was late by the time I got to the hotel so I decided to go and see Sharon in Likoni the following day. After checking in, I went to find my friend George in the bar. I sat there talking and a woman came over. "Hello, I have a message from your friend." She passed me a note.

> *Well, old man, I've done it. I took your advice and*
> *got myself an English husband. I told him if he*
> *wants me he needs to marry me, and he did. I now*
> *live in England.*
>
> *Hope you are well, old man.*
>
> *Love Madam xx*
>
> *Ps...We had fun. x*

I sat and sipped my drink, thinking about her. The last time was on the beach with the scousers, but there was another time when she did her usual 'appear from nowhere' routine and was desperate to treat me for dinner; she grabbed my hand, marching me along the beach to a place. It was St. Valentine's Day and the outside area was full of couples holding hands at candlelit tables. "I'm not bloody going there," I said, but I didn't have much choice, she literally dragged me there. The loved up couples looked over with curiosity as the old bloke with his young woman friend ate, drank and laughed together.

I was thrilled for her, so happy, but also sad that I'd never see her again.

The next day when I got to the village it was quiet. I saw people I knew but no one approached me, which in itself was unusual, they always knew I was coming and they always made a big fuss.

Friends and neighbours used to come out to meet me, waiting for their gifts. I used to buy a load of pens and sweets for the kids but today there was hardly anyone around her house. I was a day late so that must be it. I went straight to Sharon's house and was surprised to find strangers living there. It was difficult communicating, they didn't speak English and they didn't respond to my Swahili so I gave up and carried on wandering around the village looking for familiar faces, then I saw one. The Landlord coming out of his local bar saw me and came over.

I started by asking him questions; where Sharon was and who the people were in her house. He stuttered, hesitating, thinking through his reply before he spoke, acting nervous with a serious edge to his demeanour. He moved his outstretched arm behind my back, motioning me into the bar he had just come out of.

Sit down, Sir. Sit down. He knew my name so I couldn't understand the formalities and then he just came straight out with it. "Your girlfriend and your son are dead." He didn't wait for my response. "She was by the river, washing clothes, your son was playing in the water, the next moment he was gone. The river is very strong, we found him but too late."

"Sharon?"

"The next day her neighbour found her hanging." Guilt. She couldn't live with herself. She blamed herself and took her own life. She let you down. She let a mzungu down and—"

"Where are they?" I interrupted him. "Where are they buried?" "Take me, show me, show me."

I walked out of the bar, waited for him to pass and I followed. We walked out of the village and he pointed to a burial area ahead. We zig-zagged, looking down at the ground, avoiding the other graves and it wasn't long before we found it. Dogs sat around the site near patches of darkened fresh soil where the dogs had scratched earlier. The dogs hung around, not giving up, they could smell the bodies, which meant they weren't deep enough. I stood looking down at the spot, contemplating my next move then realised I was alone. The Landlord had slipped away quietly, leaving me to it, making his way back probably to the bar, which he did most afternoons. I walked to the nearest house, asked for a spade and took a wheelbarrow – mangled and misshapen with a flat tyre, that squeaked as I pushed it back to the site. I stripped to my underwear and started digging. I was leaking before I started. I reached out, grabbing, balling up my shirt and pressed it hard into my eye sockets plugging, stopping the constant flow of sweat that was burning my eyes.

I wasn't used to working in this kind of heat. The problem here was the scorched, hard-baked ground made it virtually impossible to dig deep and that's why I found them so soon – only three foot down. Whoever buried them had given up and that's why the dogs were waiting for dinner.

The heat and the exertion made me feel giddy and I stood resting, propping myself up on the handle, my skin burning, thinking I was going to faint at any second. It was the wrong time to be doing this – at midday, the sun in Kenya is a killer. Kenyans take time out from their daily routine, staying indoors, avoiding heavy work for the few hours around midday when the sun is at its hottest.

An old mzungu stripped down to his pants digging a grave at this time caused a bit of interest; I could see people, shaded from their homes, chatting, looking over at me. The cape of dust that crusted my body was now dark and stuck to my sweaty skin.

The sun hung over my head, burning into my neck and shoulders but I carried on until I saw a patch of the hessian sack in the ground.

I turned the spade around and used the other side, gently scraping away soil to reveal more of the lumpy sack. I stuck the spade back in and levered the handle quickly back and forth prising and loosening the soil under so I could lift it out of its hole.

Then the smell of death and decay seeped up from the ground. I smothered my mouth and nose with my hand but not quick enough, it was too late, that smell was inside me now. Severe pain burned at the base of my nose and my head throbbed.

As I lifted the load I could feel by the weight and see by the shape appearing that it was going to be too big to balance. Soil crumbled away as I reached down with one hand to steady the load. As I did, my fingers seared through it like wet tissue I could feel mushy rotten limbs between my fingers. I straightened and threw the spade to one side now with both hands and lifted the lot into the barrow.

I started spearing the bottom of the hole with my spade, trying to cut down deeper but it was solid and I was getting nowhere. I stood in the hole looking out and around the landscape and saw the place. A coconut tree. I knew the ground around it would be softer more fertile and that's where I laid them to rest. I squeaked away, angry. Not even fucking buried properly. I finished patting the ground hard with the back of the shovel. Job done.

I walked away reeking of death, covered in a crust of soil and sweat dust that made my eyes sting as I rubbed them. Trying to remember the next part was sketchy. I spent the next ten years trying to piece together exactly what happened. Shock must have taken over and blocked it out but I couldn't remember how I got from the grave to the hotel.

Watching a travel documentary in 2010 sparked the memory back again. It was a bloke in the sea somewhere hot, just stood in one spot cupping water over himself. That was it. That was me.

The Landlord arranged a taxi for me and I asked the driver to stop short of the hotel. I got out and walked around the outer perimeter towards the beach. I waded in, scooping water over myself, cupping with both hands as I went. I stopped at waist height and scrubbed myself. I didn't want to take the smell anywhere near the place. The sea calmed me and cleansed me of the stench of those graves.

22. Got Me!

The next two days couldn't come soon enough. I always sorted my pick up towards the end of my stay. I didn't fancy having the stuff on me any longer than needed. I had nightmares and couldn't wait to fly back and try and forget about this particular trip. It must have seemed strange to the staff, particularly George who I always had a laugh with, to see me this way. I moped around the hotel in a daze and wasn't up to socialising.

I'd spent years wanting to escape to get away and found the place of my dreams, but now after this I wanted to leave and I wasn't in a rush to come back. I was exhausted when I got to the airport, the events of the day before whirled around my head and wouldn't let me sleep. But I was ready packed and preparing for the journey home.

The flight home involved changing planes at Nairobi, that first part of the journey taking just over an hour. It was a part of the trip I'd done this journey nine times over the past four years. I knew the airport layout, the number of staff and where they would be at different times of the day. Today was very busy. When you get to the terminal at Nairobi, you have the choice to go left to end your journey or if, like me, you have a connecting flight, then you take a right. The two passengers near me were already in the queue to get off the plane but I just sat back in my seat and looked out of the window. I could see vehicles and people buzzing around outside as they prepared to attach the stairs to the plane. The airport bus pulled up and opened both its doors and waited, and it wasn't long before the first lot of passengers filled the bus. I was among the last off and tagged on to the end of the queue which was working its way to the front of the plane and the exit. Once inside the building, I followed the back of a thick crowd of people, which was drifting and funnelling at the foot of the escalator. I did think about taking the empty staircase to get there quicker but I knew speed wasn't always a good thing, so I took my time, camouflaging myself in the crowd. I felt hidden in the mass of bodies around me and when it came to my turn to step on to the escalator, I looked down, stepping out onto the moving stair and glanced up and then down again, realising something had caught my eye, but I didn't want to seem obvious so I casually looked everywhere first then back to the spot. Unusual to see faces at this stage, I thought. I got halfway up and could now see that the faces behind the glass looking down had uniforms on. I panicked. They shouldn't be there. Never once had I seen people at this point before. Maybe it was a new security measure, beefing up security wasn't out of the question. I kept coming up with different scenarios in my head, looking for answers as to why those people were there. I spent the rest of the time looking at the bloke in front, my gaze fixed on his back and his creased brown linen jacket. I could, without looking straight back at them, see movement. A quick check again and the space behind the glass was empty – panic over. I relaxed again. Nothing to do with you, Terry. I edged to the top and could see that wasn't the case. The same three people were now standing to one side smiling, acknowledging the passengers ahead of me as they got off the escalator.

"Mr Johnson." I didn't answer, hoping another Mr Johnson would answer. "Mr Johnson." I turned and deliberately kept my reactions as natural as I could, but I knew it was game over. Someone had faded the background noise and all I could hear in stereo was myself. My heart thumped loudly through my shirt.

Over the last few years I had become an expert at masking my emotions under pressure and thinking fast on my feet in so many situations. Not this time, this was the end, I could sense it, but not only that, something else happened. Normally, my mind would be buzzing, sharpening, preparing for ideas, a way out, what do I do next, Terry – that sort of thing. But this time, nothing but calmness took over me in both mind and body that I couldn't explain at the time. I was caught with drugs and facing up to ten years in prison, but I was so calm about it all. Relief and acceptance at finally being caught was maybe part of it, but now ten years on and looking back, I could see that I was still in shock. Forty-eight hours previously, I had reburied my new family and I just felt numb about everything and wanted to be as far away as possible.

"Yeh sure, what's this all about then?" I didn't even sound convincing. Other passengers started to slow up behind me, taking an interest in my situation.

The older shorter bloke was holding a card. They didn't answer and a loaded mini truck was conveniently parked up nearby, and I was asked to pick my case, which I did. "We need to see in your case, Sir," said the woman.

I was then taken to a room made of a flimsy timber frame; it looked bendy and fragile like a poorly built summerhouse that had survived a few storms with no roof and a perspex window. This was their office and it stuck out from the rest of the airport by its shabbiness. They sat me at a desk that was overloaded with paperwork, and potted plants so dry the soil had shrunk away from the sides and were shrivelled, drooping over the sides. The two blokes virtually ignored me for the first ten minutes and stood at one end with my case picking through it, casually chatting to each other in Swahili. I understood a bit, a shop murder and robbery and something about his wife and her car which was being repaired. I took in my surroundings; it wasn't just the desk, there were boxes stuffed with paper stacked high around the room, it was unorganised and chaotic. I sat feeling unfazed and fully accepting my situation. I sat there in complete calmness, I dropped all my defences that I had intuitively had at airports. I'd been caught good and proper. The woman who caught me came back in and started leafing through a box of paperwork and I asked her for a coffee. She told me they didn't have a kettle, couldn't afford one and then I just came out with it.

"One day," I said, "in the future when I come back through this airport I will bring you kettle. Ok?" I have no idea why I said that. I was caught with three kilos in her airport, I wasn't sure what I was going to face, possibly up to ten years…and I promised to buy her a fucking kettle.

She looked at me as though I'd lost the plot but smiled anyway. "Yeh right, I will keep you to that," she said.

The short bloke holding the card was now holding aloft my dark cling filmed package. The card had my description on it, I didn't get a proper look but it was good enough to catch me. I wasn't just a random search, they had been waiting for me.

"Mr Johnson, this is serious." He held the package, waving it to and fro as he spoke. I just sat there and agreed, nodding every time he spoke. I sat in silence watching him as he walked the floor area like a headmaster with his hands behind his back.

"Ten years. Ten years." He kept reminding me. "You are an old man, this will be tough for you, ten years here in Africa. An African prison is not a good place to be, people die."

They left me alone for a while and seemed to get on with other things then surprised me. "You hungry, Mr Johnson?" He stood up and opened the door wide. "Come, come with us and eat." They took me to their staff canteen on the second floor and we ate together. They chatted away while I tucked into a plate of chips and about half an hour later I was back in the office and he got straight to the point.

"Mr Johnson, if you pay us £500 you are free to go. A free man."

"Get stuffed," was my reaction. I knew about this scam so always kept a few hundred on me just in case, but this time I had about a tenner and some loose change.

"Ok, ok three hundred. Three hundred pounds and you are a free man." I shook my head.

"Come on, in England this is nothing, you give it to me and you are free."

133

I kept telling them I had no money, I even gestured by pulling out the pocket lining of my trousers and opening my wallet but they continued asking.

"Your family. They will help, yeh? Your family, ask them for money, we can wait." Nope I have no family. Who will pay? I felt ashamed, I didn't want to ask my family. I was prepared to take the ten years. This was the surest sign I wasn't thanking straight. One call to my sister in Canada would have been easy but the truth is, I did feel ashamed, shell-shocked about everything that had happened. This was my mess and I was going to get myself out of it, and if that meant not paying the corrupt police, then so be it.

23. Mozzies and Remand

I didn't ask and they didn't tell me, but after a short drive from the main terminal and still within the confines of the airport, we came to the Police station. It stood alone, higher and more impressive-looking than anything around with a carved stone columned entrance.

The copper/desk sergeant stood up from his worn leather seat, the foam filling bulging out of the split at one side. He took a broken biro and started writing.

Signed in and searched I was then taken to a cell, one of four where I spent the next three nights. Alone. That same night a thick cluster of mosquitoes came in through the grilled window so I sat huddled up, knees tight to my chest and wrapped the blanket around me the best I could, covering, shielding myself but kept waking to find myself half-covered and bitten. Sometime later, the clanking of the gate woke me again and the same two male airport cops came into my cell, one of them was carrying a burner which he hung and told me it would make the mosquitoes dopey and less aggressive.

"When you get back to England, tell them about two kind po-licemen, ok?" Didn't sound like a joke and if he was serious not sure why he said it.

They both came later that morning and took me back to the airport which surprised me. I wasn't handcuffed and we sat near where I was first arrested and watched travellers as they passed by. I wasn't sure why; maybe they wanted me to run, I don't know, but I just stayed with them for what must have been about six or seven hours and at the end of their shift they took me back to the station for another night in the cell.

The following day, the 29th January 2001, was my sixtieth birthday and I was taken to court and then sent to remand to await my trial. Remand Prison; Nairobi.

The cell I shared with fourteen others measured roughly the size of my living room (16x10). One small grilled opening in the wall gave us light, a tap gave us water and a bucket on a rope fixed to the wall was the toilet. No beds. We all had patches of material which we all mapped to the floor as our bed space.

That first morning was one I'll never forget. When I did eventually fall asleep I opened my eyes again and my first reaction was a wetness that covered one side of me, then the smell. I felt suffocated by the stench of humans tangled around me and realised in a split second why the smell was so strong. The bloke next to me had turned around in his sleep and not made the bucket. My hands, face and the one side I slept on, were smothered in his shit.

The next problem I had was the water, or lack of it. There was no set time for us to have water. The askaris (guards) would turn the water on whenever they felt liked it. They did this throughout my time in prison and the time you waited for it to come back on depended on the individual askari and his mood that day.

All I wanted to do was get to that tap and scrub myself down but I couldn't. The morning sun outside got hotter, making the cell and the smell in it even worse. It was horrendous. Welcome to remand..

All meals were served outside on the grass and the main ingredient in my diet was ugali (maize) and water and it featured on the menu a lot.

Breakfast: ugali, made to a thin soup consistency.

Lunch: ugali, but a bit thicker, like custard with Sukuma wiki which is a very strong Kale used to feed cattle. It's hard to digest but is popular with poor people as it's very cheap. The phrase 'Sukuma Wiki' translates as 'get through the week' and gives people enough energy to literally get through the week.

Meat arrived twice a week and they brought it into the cell on a tin tray, which everyone dived for. Now unlike my younger cellmates I wore dentures and this meat was very salty and leathery tough. It took me ages to chew the first mouthful, by which time the others had eaten the fucking lot. I got wise to this so when the meat came around I took a big handful, they all started on me, so I explained about their clear advantage and they left me alone in the corner to eat. They got it back anyway. Excessive use of my jaw throbbed with pain so in the end I gave up trying to chew it, gave it away and just went hungry. I never did find out what type of meat it was. I asked a few times but no one knew, no one cared, they just wolfed it down like dogs.

I did find out how the meat came to us.

I heard the sound of an engine one day so I leapt up to the window which overlooked the compound. A battered red Toyota pick-up skidded into the compound, throwing up a plume of dust. Two guys got out, unhinged and dropped the back end down, pulled the dust sheet away that was stretched over the back and grabbed the tied legs of each carcass, lifting, jerking them onto one shoulder and carried them inside. I counted six in total and not one of them was covered. Forget vacuum packing and refrigeration, that's how it came in but I never knew what I was eating, still don't today.

I couldn't cope with the food and refused the meat, I just couldn't chew it and the greens tasted bitter. That left the maize but even that gave me chronic stomach pains. In the end I refused all meals.

One cellmate could see I wasn't eating and gave me some words of wisdom. "Hey, the food ain't going to get better so why don't you get it anyway and swap for cigarettes." Good idea.

After the first week, I could see the frame of my body shrinking with weight loss. One week is a long time without food and as each day passed I felt weaker and weaker, and unstable on my feet. The guards ignored me at first, thought I was faking it. I didn't fully pass out but I felt faint as if I was going down, my knees would buckle and it felt like I was going to collapse, so I used to go down to the floor, get on my hands and knees to steady myself then I'd try to stand back up.

We all had to line up outside for our food. One day I actually forced myself to eat just to give me strength and was on my way back inside when I saw one of the lads in charge picking food up off the floor; he had a lump of food in one hand the size of a cricket ball; I asked him what it was for.

"Him over there, he's starving," he said, and this bony figure appeared down the fence waiting for his food.

The next day, the sergeant came in, we all had to stand to attention, and he did a double take when he saw me. "Ahh, a mzungu, not very often we have a mzungu here."

I just blurted it out. "Look Sir, I've not eaten for a week now, it's my stomach, I can't eat the food here. I'm not used to it." He just told me I had to see the doctor. I saw the doctor who had a couple of officials with him. They all laughed and seemed to think it was a big joke.

"Our food not good enough for you, mzungu, eh?" After they mocked me they sent me to my cell and I actually thought I was going to starve to death. I felt so weak, so frail.

Askari's brought the food over but every now and again a sergeant would bring mine over personally. As soon as I saw him coming with it, I knew it was going to cost me. I had a kitty for toiletries and essentials, which my family sent me, and he wanted some of it. I never said no.

24. England v Germany

My health was deteriorating by the day. My limbs ached and a pain in both ears was getting worse every day, so I asked the guard if I could see a doctor. Two days later, I was released and taken over the other side of the compound. It was a nice green area with lots of planted flowerbeds.

I found a large crowd of people pushing; guards waded in, beating them back with sticks; it was chaos. I got talking to a tall gangly bloke in front of me.

"It's always the same when the doctor comes," he said. I noticed most of his body was covered in sores. As I got closer I could see someone sat at a table in the middle of the yard; it looked like an old bank manager's desk – solid with thick carved legs. They crowded around the doctor who held something shiny in his hand, he held it up, taking a closer look at it.

The bloke I'd been speaking to moments before walked back after seeing the doctor, opened his hand and showed me an aspirin. This man was a walking open wound and all he got was fucking aspirin. Fuck that. I walked back over and decided to wait for my next day in court. I found out the shiny thing in his hand was a silver watch which kept him busy haggling with his customers/patients.

I told the lady judge about my ears and asked her for permission to go to hospital and see a proper doctor.

She listened and started writing and summed up the hearing. "Yes, Mr Johnson needs to go to hospital." She looked down, ticking her paper. "Yes, yes, that's ok, I've made a note of all this."

When the day came two guards came to collect me in an old jeep. They all just stared at me as I walked through Nairobi

General Hospital; I was used to that. An old white man handcuffed to the two guards was a novelty for them.

To start with he seemed to know what he was talking about. He told me my ears weren't balanced properly. I told him I had a problem flying and he inspected both ears. "Gum," he said, "you need gum."

"Gum?"

"Chewing gum," he said and started to give me a clue by pretending to chew himself. "Chewing gum, you know." No ear drops or painkillers. Unbelievable. I should have seen the prison doctor, could have sold my gold filling. So I just had to chew gum, but first I needed permission.

The sergeant was next door at the time and two gates separated us from where he was, and I was stopped and searched at each one. When I got there I sensed a different mood from these prisoners, straight away the guards did as well, they flanked me either side and gripped their batons the whole time we were there.

As soon as they saw me the small groups all merged together, about forty of them, all watching me. It was strange to see them in blue stripes; we had no uniform really, just a mismatch of clothes. The guards drew their batons and shouted orders and they stepped back slowly, creating a path through the crowd. I could feel their eyes burning into me, the whole time the atmosphere was menacing and volatile.

We found the sergeant at the end of the yard. He was sat against the wall in the shade, playing draughts. I stood to attention before him, not looking down. He was busy in conversation chatting to the other guards so I waited and chose my moment to talk.

"Sir, I've been to the hospital today about my ears and the doctor said I need to chew gum so I've come here to ask your permission to chew gum, Sir."

He took his time deliberating over his next move and when he finished he spoke.

"Yes." Turning to the other guards with me, "Let it be known Mr Johnson can chew gum."

I thanked him and we made the uncomfortable walk back. The crowd was even more intimidating and purposely blocked our route back, which encouraged the guards to draw their batons again, forcing the crowd to spread out, and leaving us to march quickly to the gate.

I soon got to know the guards on duty and their different personalities, good and bad. Most of the officers were more educated and spoke very good English, one in particular surprised me on several occasions with his knowledge of British History, especially both World Wars. He'd search me out in the exercise yard and tell me random trivia about Churchill and Hitler. He was always polite and addressed me by my name instead of just 'mzungu'. He liked the fact I was British and it gave him the chance to show off a bit.

One day, he came in and ordered me out of my cell. "Mr Johnson, I've got someone outside who wants to meet you." He led me out into the yard. "Here you are, he's just come in today and goes to court tomorrow and it's likely he'll go home, but first we need to find a few things out." I could tell by his vagueness this wasn't going to be good.

A German bloke in his forties sat waiting for us. The guard took his place between us on the kerb stone.

"This man is from Germany." Then, turning to me, he said, "and this man is from England." I knew where this was going.

"Right, I want to talk about the war, the Second World War."

Oh god here we go. The first question was for me.

"What do you think of those bloody Germans, exterminating all those Jews, eh? Mmm? What's your opinion?"

He looked at me, staring into my face, waiting for my answer. "Well, that's all in the past as far as I'm concerned." I just answered the best I could in a polite way so as not to upset the German who could hear every word.

He turned to the German. He didn't just twist my answer, he made his own up and retold it to the German. He said, pausing while thinking of what to say, "You fucking Germans are cruel bastards, what d'you say about that?" I leant slightly forward and could see this poor guy's expression as he stumbled his words unsure of what to say. His English wasn't good but I could read the discomfort on his face and, like me, he understood the situation of what this guard was trying to do.

"Sorry, sorry, long time before I'm sorry."

Now straight back to me. "What about your country, and London they bombed the shit out of your city, how do you feel about this?" I gave my answer diplomatically, he changed it and would tell the German something totally different and so the game went on. He would always start by saying, "He said..." and whatever bullshit words he made up would follow.

"He said, 'You fucking Germans are fucking animals', what do you say to that?" This poor German looked at the sergeant and looked at me, unsure how to answer.

The whole premise was surreal. A kind of England vs. Germany quiz, but the aim of the Quizmaster who made the rules up as he went along, was to get us angry so we'd start fighting each other.

After a while he gave up, he could tell it wasn't going to plan. He stood up and announced for us to shake hands and return back to our cells. No World War Three today.

That German in remand was the only white face I saw there but that wasn't the case in my next prison, there I was definitely the only white man.

25. The Man with No Face

Now it's fair to say the guards like a drink or a spliff, and some turn up for work smashed out of their skulls. One time this happened it left me with nightmares for weeks after.

It was early evening and we'd just been fed and locked up as usual. Then I heard it, a single piercing scream at first which made me jump, and this scream turned to prolonged shouting which got louder. I felt the pain, the agony in that first piercing scream that I'll never forget. The noise got louder and closer until I heard the clanking of the corridor gate open. I moved to the bars to see a man screaming on the floor of our corridor, the guards pushed him there and locked the gate behind him.

Now on his knees, unable to take his hands away from his face, he still made a noise which seemed to echo throughout the building. He quickly got up and raced to each cell shouting, pleading for help. I stepped forward, straining to get a better look through the bars and could see he was at the other end working his way towards my cell. I moved back into my cell, sensing he was near, unsure what to expect. Like a jumpy scene in a horror movie he appeared in front of me and removed his hands from the face he was holding. It was pure horror. I've never seen anything like it in my life and I hope I never will again.

Skin on his face and shoulders had peeled off. The only way I can describe this poor, poor man's face was like a tomato that had been plunged into boiling, scalding water, the loose folds of skin, curled up from the heat were now peeled back and hanging off. It was like watching a victim of a slasher movie – only this one was real. His face was completely raw and bloodied.

His bloodshot eyes bulged with pain searching our cell, darting around at me and the others hoping someone, anyone could help him stop the excruciating pain he was in. He was gone again but when he reappeared his noise was different, his screams were now a painful whimper.

He was quiet now, almost whispering, looking like he would pass out at any moment.

"Help me," he said. "Jesus, help me."

I shouted, the other guys with me made a racket, banging, making as much noise as we could, hoping for a guard to help this tragic bloke. He kept running back and forth to each cell, reappearing at mine through the bars and kept repeating the same thing. Delirious and now clearly hallucinating, he pointed at me, calling me Jesus. "Jesus please. Jesus, help me."

I was the only white face there and with my beard I think he actually thought I was Jesus.

I've never seen a human being suffer pain like this. I sat back down, lifted a blanket over my head and just blocked it all out. I found all this too much to cope with. I was helpless, the guards eventually came and took him away.

The corporal in charge on that shift had been drinking the famous Changaa. The same stuff I tried in Loitoktok. The screaming man was on the loo at the time when the guards, under orders from the boozed/drugged up officer, poured a pot of boiling water over his head. I never did know that poor bugger's name. I still get upset even now when I think about it; I felt totally useless and desperately wanted to help him. His ripped apart bleeding face is etched on my mind. He was eventually taken to hospital but never returned to prison. A pardon was issued after human rights got involved. This was unusual. I saw many brutal things in prison which were never reported; they always did their best to cover their tracks, especially where I was involved. I had links with the British embassy and human rights; they tried to cover up but I still saw too much of what was going on.

I'd seen many askaris start the nightshift drunk. They never seemed to have a problem getting through the main gate. Many of them, mainly the same ones, could get drunk or stoned for a few shillings. Tembo wine is popular too. Tembo, or Elephant wine, as they call it is made from a coconut tree. Farmers tap the sap from the palm that normally goes to form a coconut, they leave it to naturally ferment but it's got to be drunk fairly quickly as it turns sour if it's left too long. They make it at home and leave it to ferment, and nearly every time I'd been to someone's home I was offered Tembo. They make it for special occasions, like weddings and birthdays.

Beatings took place on a regular basis in remand and it depended on the mood of the askari. Some were nasty even if they weren't drunk or high on drugs. One spot of sober cruelty was when I was in court; as I was escorted from the cell to the courtroom, a man with no legs came towards us, literally swinging on his arms. As he went past, one of the other guards lunged out and kicked him over, sending him flying. You bastard, I thought.

26. Court

Whilst in remand, I went to court four times before my final sentencing, and it was the same lady judge. Court wasn't a problem, it was just how I got there.

The guards came to my cell at about seven in the morning and I was herded with all the others into a waiting cell. Somebody would come out and shout and we'd all filter slowly to the reception area and wait for our money. My money for court was put into my pocket minus the deduction for the guard on duty and we would spend the next hour waiting.

It didn't matter what size lorry turned up, it was never big enough. Between the drivers and us was a steel framed box with seats where four guards sat with their AK47s. The back of the lorry had see-through slats for the lucky ones who found themselves squashed against them; at least they had air which the ones jammed in the middle didn't have.

We were funnelled into the back; pushed, kicked and shoved and the last ones were beaten to get everyone in. Once in, you couldn't move, jammed and tangled up with bodies I found it hard to breathe. The end of this two-hour journey was a huge relief for everyone. We all climbed out, gulping the air and stretching our limbs in the sunshine. Extra guards came out and formed a circle around us and the lorry where we stood to be counted.

The court building looked more like a palace. Impressive stone arches at the entrance with giant columns and balcony over it. We were taken single file through the door and downstairs into the cells. On the left side of the building as you went in was a large cellar-type room, dark with a low ceiling, fitted with shelves. A dusty old place with suitcases, bags, tagged with names and numbers. I remember being taken there because the judge on one occasion said to me, "Mr Johnson, I'm fed up of seeing you with the same red shirt on." At the time I thought her statement was incredible.

What's going on here then? I thought. Is she my bloody mother, or what? It's a court case, why the concern for my clothes? The other blokes I was chained to were all in rags, but she thought it was important enough to break for fifteen minutes so I could find my case in the dusty cloakroom, all because she was fed up with the colour of my shirt. So I was taken to the reception and told the girl what I wanted and she wrote it down, I signed and then it took her five minutes or so to find my suitcase and when then did, they opened it and found everything in it was covered in furry green mould.

I went back to the court and she asked me why I hadn't changed. I told her and she had no choice, she had to put up with my red shirt. I never did get my case back – not that it was worth it.

That first time in court, I didn't think about taking money with me, something I soon regretted when a bloke pointed out the obvious. "Not much room in here is there? Have you got any money?"

"Not with me."

I started to worry why he was asking but then he explained. "Ok, the next time, bring a hundred bob, let the guard know and see what that gets you."

Prisoners were allowed to have money in remand and it was handy on court day, but to get it you either had to tell the man in charge he could have some of it or pay him on the spot.

Money my family sent went straight to the British embassy in Nairobi, and once a month an official visited me to check my welfare and gave the Officer in Charge money for things I needed – toiletries, soap, etc. but that was the problem. They were better off buying me these essentials, which I would have taken straight to my cell. Instead, the money was held in a kitty and trying to get any of it was hard work and when I did the guards wanted their cut most of the time and helped themselves.

So to ensure my next visit to court would be more comfortable I started taking money.

As soon as I got the chance I showed the guard my hundred shillings, he nodded and told me to stay exactly where I stood, while he made sure others filled the remaining cells. He took my money and pointed to an empty cell which was waiting for me, he nodded, gesturing me to go into it. Unlike the last time I had this cell to myself, he left the door wide open and even had my own newspaper to read, (three months old) but it felt like luxury just being able to read something. All I needed now was a taxi back to remand.

Another court appearance and the usual thing, being hand-cuffed in pairs, we were led underneath the courts and into the cells. Those without money were all pushed together into one cell. I was in another cell with about three or four others because I'd taken advice and brought money with me that time too. The askari told me to follow him down the corridor and he opened the office door to a table full of food and introduced me to his family standing around it, leaving me to it and closing the door behind him.

I joined the table with the lucky others fortunate to have paid the guard and had already made a start. We all feasted on this spread of mouth watering brightly-coloured Arabic and Indian food. I was only allowed five minutes so I stuffed myself silly until I heard the door open. Time up, and I was taken back to the cell. This guard had a good little side-line and a way to earn a few bob, getting his family in with food and collecting money off those who could afford the private banquet.

Askaris always looked for ways to make a bit more money because their wages were so low. On busy court days they would allow street vendors into each cell, selling bread, cakes, cigarettes and drinks.

The guard would take his cut of the sales and everyone was happy. One scam I got to know was the "I'll get your change later" scam. The askari informed the vendor which prisoners were not coming back to court – the ones who were to be sentenced.

It worked when these prisoners handed over a note requiring change, the vendors would tell them they didn't have change and as soon as they did they would come and find them. They never did. The change would be split between the askari and the vendor.

When it was time to leave court, we'd all get into that familiar position of squatting down and waiting. Those that had been before knew better, they knew the drill here and the top tip was to make sure you spent all your money in court and took nothing back to prison as it would only get taken off you by the guards, and if you complained, you got beaten. Those askaris were something else, they were like vultures in Jack boots. Same procedure; when you got back around half-seven at night, the bit of money you had left you'd hand back to the guard and then you were herded into another yard with a new set of askaris who had one thing on their minds. Money. They didn't just search you, they lifted you off the ground and shook every fucking shilling they could find on you out onto the floor. By the time we were back to the cell gate of our block and it could be as late as nine o'clock, we were made to wait a further ten minutes for them to get around to opening the gate.

They kept the food back while you were in court, but it was even less appetising when it was cold, it took on another form; a gluey, gloopy consistency which was hard to palate so I never used to eat mine if it was cold. They'd take mine away and keep it for the following day; the Boy in Charge would pass the same food back through a hole in the fence.

27. Potatoes

My own health was getting worse, I was getting weaker and they continued to ignore my request for the food to change so I waited till the next embassy meeting with Jill.

She could see just by looking at me things were not good.

"I'm going to starve to death here," I told her.

"I've told them I can't eat this food." The officer looked shocked and embarrassed in front of Jill and played out the part for her benefit.

"Mr Johnson, have they not done this for you?" he said, knowing full well they hadn't. He interrupted us and pretended to take an interest. I told her what I'd been surviving on and she turned to the Officer in Charge.

"Right. Mr Johnson needs to have bread, potatoes and milk added to his diet with immediate effect."

"Yes Madam."

"Take note of this," he said to the askari by the door, flexing his power a bit and replayed the order and told him he was responsible for my extra food.

Potatoes turned up first later that day, but what a farce that was. The cells were only opened at certain times of the day and my new diet Guru would turn up with my potatoes at just the right time (well from their point of view) and that would, of course, be when I was locked in the cell. Unable to break the rules and open my cell to give me my spuds, they left the pot outside the bars making sure they were just out of my reach. Bastards.

I'd sit on the floor and wait for the doors to open, just the bars separating me from my spuds, guarding them the best I could.

"Oi, fucking leave my spuds alone!" The guards would take it in turns walking past, swooping down to nick a potato or two as they went by, leaving me watching on, helpless.

When they did open my cell I used to share them around with the boys anyway. The milk was a joke as well. I was allowed one glass a day and what I got was a warm watery solution. The kitchen staff sold our milk and it was a nice little side-line for them, then they would top it back up with water. I did the test and left my glass full overnight and in the morning the water, which was most of it, had now separated from the milk.

It didn't take me long for my body to respond to the extra food and after three or four days, I started to feel physically stronger and my mind sharpened up as I questioned how I was going to get through all this.

When I was finally sentenced, I was taken up from the cells as usual but this time I went into court number one. A gate at the bottom with very steep stairs led up to the back of the court. I could see the judge and prisoners waiting to go in and an open side door where the general public were free to casually roam in and out of the courtroom.

The same lady judge as before sat at a desk at the top with a raised box to one side and four steps down. Six of us stood chained together in a line and waited for the next person's case to end, and when it did, we all shuffled to the left. The judge called his name and the guy I was chained with answered and moved into position and looked up to the judge as she called out his name and read his charges.

"Would you like to mitigate or say something before I pass sentence on you?" she asked. I didn't understand his reply but the way he said it, his expression and the judge's reaction, it wasn't very polite.

She slammed the gavel down and doubled his sentence with two extra strokes for his insult. The lads told me later that he more or less told her to get stuffed.

My turn in front of the lady judge. I was asked the same thing. What I said, I had spent the last couple of days rehearsing. This is the same judge who allowed me to go to hospital because of my ears. She also gave me the chance to change from that red shirt I was wearing, so I got the feeling she had a bit of a soft spot for me and maybe being British played a big part in that as well. So here I was, facing up to ten years. I stood up, stepped forward and said, "Ma'am. I have brought shame on myself, my family and I want to make it very clear to you and this court today that I have learnt my lesson and you will never see me here ever again."

I stepped back, looked down to the floor, keeping my eyes there, and I waited.

My head bowed, I stared at my feet and started counting to myself. I got to twelve seconds. It seemed like ages then she spoke. "One year," and slammed the gavel down again. I thanked the Judge and left court feeling very happy. I couldn't believe the outcome; I was expecting five or six years. She could have made an example of me – a white British citizen committing a crime in her country, breaking the law, which she as a judge upheld. I was extremely lucky to get a decision like that. Maybe she did have a soft spot for me after all.

In the last few days of remand, they told me which prison I was going to, and when the boys found out, they tried to console me. "I'm sorry, fancy sending you there."

One lad came across and gave me his soap and other things to take. "I'm sorry to hear this, good luck."

The day before I left remand I took exercise for what would be my last time walking, circling the yard. Then I stopped to cool off and did my usual thing and stood in a shaded part. I used to find the same piece of wire that stuck out from the stone wall and stand there on a raised rock holding the end of it, holding and balancing at the same time. Then four or five askaris came in, looking menacing, tapping their batons in their palm and looking for a victim. One shouted at me, ordering me down. I just ignored him and looked the other way. The other prisoners had now stopped their circling and were lined up near the door and watched me disobey his order. He nodded at the other guard, who reeked of alcohol, to step forward, which he did and brought down his stick across my fingers. Pain seared through my hand and up my arm and I instantly let go of the wire. This was the first and only time I'd ever been hit and it shocked me; I went straight to his face, boiling with anger.

"If you ever EVER, do that again, I'll take that stick and ram it down your fucking throat." He stared widely at me, he was much younger, much stronger than I was but he could see the conviction and the rage in my expression that I wasn't scared of him, and realising he had more to lose, he backed down.

When I first went to remand I feared everyone; I was after all the only white man in a black man's prison. It was a shock to the system being in a place like that. I felt vulnerable – a target – I feared everyone and felt weak in my mind and was getting weaker by the day in my body. It sounds dramatic but I thought my life would finish in an African jail.

As soon as my food changed, I got stronger by the day and my mind opened up again, buzzing with thoughts. It didn't take long but as time went on I realised they feared me, not physically, but what I stood for, who I represented. I was a British citizen serving time in the Commonwealth country of Kenya and had monthly connections with the British embassy who ensured my human rights. I was lucky, most Kenyans, especially the poor, do not have any rights or connection with the outside world and in some cases, as I witnessed time and time again, a total abuse and abandonment of basic human rights. The guy who'd hit me that day realised he'd made a mistake – in fact, the following day he apologised.

Towards the end of remand my confidence came back. I understood the African prison system and learnt to play it. Four months of constant overcrowded, hot conditions, mashed together waking, breathing and sleeping in the same putrid stench was unbearable. I was glad to leave but nervous about where I was going.

28. Hotel Kamiti

Twelve months in Africa's notorious Kamiti Prison. Handcuffed in pairs, we were led out and into a waiting van. We sat in the back, four on each side handcuffed together, and all I could do was close my eyes. It was hard to clear my mind of home and England but I knew if I was going to get through it I had to block out my past and focus on the next year.

As soon as we pulled away, one of the other prisoners opposite started to mutter in English. I'm not sure if he was doing it for my benefit it but he was saying the alphabet. I ignored him at first, but his constant droning started to get to me, he kept on saying it over and over but missing the same letter out. I couldn't stand it any longer, I had to say something.

"V," I said.

"What?" he looked surprised.

"The letter is 'V'. You miss it out every time. S, T, U... V."

"B?"

"No. V." I repeated it slowly, emphasising the letter with my mouth.

"V...ah," he said, realising and smiling, and then started again. He carried on saying it but at least he was saying the 'V'.

"Thank you," he said.

"No problem," I said and closed my eyes again. I didn't open them for a while but when I did, I looked at this man opposite again.

"Try this," I said. I said the alphabet backwards in about seven seconds. I learnt it years ago; my record is five seconds. I repeated it, playing this bloke at his own game and getting his attention as I rambled over and over.

"Your turn."

I could tell he was confused so I said it again a lot slower then I closed my eyes again and I could hear him practise, muttering away at it backwards. I didn't only say it fast backwards but I knew all the corresponding numbers of the alphabet. People at work used to test me and shout random letters and I would answer with the relevant number at speed.

I did it with a bank clerk in Mombasa on my second holiday in Kenya. It was with Ann and we had money I needed to deposit into Barclays so we took a taxi into Mombasa. This particular occasion I wasn't robbed.

When it was my turn at the glass partition, I passed my money and book into the sunken tray and I noticed the woman had 'Demaris' on her name badge. She started counting the cash.

"Four, five, thirteen, one, eighteen, nineteen," I said quickly. She looked up with confusion and didn't have a clue what I was on about.

"Your name in numbers," I said, nodding to her badge.

She carried on with the transaction still not knowing what the hell I was on about.

"Your name in numbers," I repeated.

She gave me a receipt, still thinking about what I'd said and with her thumb and finger she lifted the bottom of her name badge and could see her working each letter out as I left.

"Goodbye." I took a quick glance back and she was still looking at her name badge, she looked up and smiled.

The bumps in the road jolted me into opening my eyes. I had dozed and woken again as we turned off the main road. The driveway to the prison was flanked with tin roofed shacks where the guards and their families lived. It was a purpose-built village with a community feel; a church, school and post office. We stopped short of two heavy gates with guarded watchtowers either side.

The lorry moved slowly in and the gates locked behind us and waited for the ones in front to open – it was a holding pen for extra security. We all emptied out and the driver shouted and we all got down on our haunches.

More askaris appeared and started heckling us, laughing to each other. A sergeant called Chui lunged forward with his stick, swiping at the guy next to me, kicking him hard to the floor – apparently he wasn't crouching low enough. 'Chui' is Swahili for 'leopard' and I soon got to know why they called him this – everyone feared him. He was, as I saw over time, a real nasty piece of work.

A sergeant older than the rest interrupted the beating. Chui looked up, his face was near mine, distorted with rage, eyes glaring and his breath reeked. He was frightening. He didn't take orders from another sergeant and didn't want to back down in front of us but he did – reluctantly, because the other sergeant ushered him away, quietly talking and looking back at us as they walked. I wondered then if their chat had anything to do with me. Again, I got the same feelings as I did in remand from time to time they tried their best to cover things up, hide things away from me. In this instance, this evil bastard had dropped his guard, was beating this poor bloke right in front of me until the other sergeant reminded him of my presence. I don't know for sure, but I don't think Chui would have been interrupted like that if I wasn't around. He didn't like me from that day onwards, and up until then he was an unstoppable force, but with me around he had to be careful.

We stayed crouched for about twenty minutes until we were eventually counted.

"This is it," one said. "Your holiday starts here, welcome to Hotel Kamiti."

The prison was originally called Kamiti Downs and was built on 1200 acres of farmland which was where some of the prisoners worked.

The prison was organised and modelled on our British Army in the 1950s with the same attitude, discipline and brutal regime.

The First Officer in Charge was the boss, the Governor and everyone below him was corrupt, but as soon as you got to his position you had to be whiter than white – honest and fair at all times. The Second Officer in Charge was his understudy, followed by sergeants and corporals.

The ordinary guards were known as askaris, or guards; they were like our squaddies.

It takes two years at college to become qualified and it's here they are taught how to deal with rapists and murderers in a fair and considerate manner, reporting to their superiors if problems arise. These, in theory, are the guidelines of a career in the prison service but as I witnessed, it was far from true. Every successful graduate gets a hundred thousand shilling loan from the prison to pay for this education; it is a lot of money to most young Kenyans and most squander it on booze and drugs. The loan is then deducted from their wages which are only 30 to 40 pounds a month and leaves them next to nothing to survive, particularly if they have a family, so as I found out, they become very clever and rely heavily on scamming the prisoners as a way of topping up their income and they would do this at any given opportunity.

Scamming the prisoners was one thing but abusing and mistreating them was another.

The guards who made the prisoners' lives hell didn't leave the prison for their own safety. The nasty bastards are never forgotten. Once a guard with a history of violence towards prisoners is seen outside prison by ex-inmates then he's in trouble. One was spotted with his wife at the time, browsing around the shops in Nairobi. They were both jumped and bundled into the back of a waiting van and taken away for a beating. They broke his arm and leg, beat him to a pulp, gouged his eye from his socket, leaving him with the other so he could watch while they took turns raping his wife.

So that's why they didn't leave. It was a life sentence for them as well.

We were taken around the main office in the compound. The askari motioned with his hands and we all stood up and were ordered to strip naked, then two guards approached us with a plastic tub; it looked heavy by the way they staggered over with it, the water sloshed to and fro, swilling over the sides. The rest waited for them to slam it to the floor and circled around it. They got up to their elbows in water and began pulling lumps of wet cloth out and like some bizarre Japanese game show, they started throwing stinking dirty clothes at us. After about five minutes the same considerate sergeant as before gave the order to stop; he looked at me and said, "Here, put these on," and handed me old but dry clothes. I guess he felt sorry for me and for a moment wanted to restore my dignity, which was kind.

The clothes I had been wearing and the last few Kenyan pounds I had in my pocket were taken and I was given a dark denim uniform and flip flops to wear.

Whenever I hear flips flops to this day, it takes me back to prison. First thing in morning and on opening the doors I would hear the sound of flip flops echo through the building. Flip flops – loads of them, like an orchestra of flip flops slapping the concrete floor as we all shuffled around like penguins to slop out.

I was issued with my uniform and flip flops and it was off to Camp David.

29. Camp David

Now let's get one thing straight; Camp David was nothing like the President's country retreat. I knew that when they told me I was going there. It was an Army-style hut – large, rectangular in shape, timber built with a pitched roof. The ground floor space was crammed with well-used foam mats, flimsy and crusted with all sorts of stains. This was my bed for the next week. There was a standpipe at one end and alongside it a hole in the floor for the toilet.

"I bet the President looks forward to coming here," I said, making those around me laugh.

In turn they came up to me and asked me questions; where I'd been, what I'd done – I was a novelty – an old white man in an African prison, and they were desperate to know my story.

The sergeant asked me if I was good at gardening. I answered positively but didn't want to appear too keen as I'm sure this was supposed to be a punishment.

"Well, you're going to cut grass tomorrow."

"That's no problem, I've done a bit of gardening in my time."

By his smirk I knew there was more to it. "By hand." Lifting his hand in front of my face he wiggled his fingers. "With these."

"No problem." And that's how I spent my first week at Camp David, cutting grass with my fingers. Ah well, first time for everything, Terry.

The large patch of grass I worked on surrounded Camp David and the next hut along was separated by a tall hedge which I purposely kept close to because every day I could hear raised voices followed by screams and was determined to find out more. The hedge was dense and too high but I managed to find a gap and when our guard wasn't looking I quickly peered through it. Young lads about eighteen or nineteen in a line up were being beaten with sticks. The force of their sticks hammering into their bodies actually made me shudder, so I quickly crouched back down to my grass cutting position before the guards could see me. I later found out that the other side of the hedge was where they kept the young offenders.

I got to know very soon that like remand this place made and changed rules as it went along so it was no surprise when I found out much later that Kamiti had a history of ignorance towards human rights issues and had become notorious as one of Africa's toughest prisons.

I realised that if I was going to get through this I would have to forget England and focus on getting through each day. I can do this, I thought.

When my mood was low, to pick myself up, I spent a few minutes most days trying to visualise the end of my sentence. I'd picture myself at the gate on my last day, collecting my things, saying good-bye, walking out of the main gate into fresh air and I ended the sequence in my head by looking up, thanking the sky that I was free.

There were about fifty of us together in Camp David. Most I'd never seen before, even the ones who were on remand with me I had trouble recognising. One day this bloke came up to me. "Hey, remember me?" It was at the end of the day, we all gathered outside, bent down on our haunches ready to be counted back in for the night. "I was in remand with you." The bloke squatted next to me whispered, keeping one eye on the guard who was busy counting moving up down the rows with his chalkboard.

I nodded but didn't have a clue who he was, but then I re-membered him as he talked.

"That guy you were with in remand, you know, the one that had a rich family."

I remembered. He was the one who told the judge to get lost and she doubled his sentence. "Well, his family paid a thousand pounds to the judge and they let him go, well he was released, within four hours they shot him dead."

"Who shot him?"

"Don't know."

No one knows who but he was involved in drugs big time so it could have been revenge from a rival gang or even the police; the fact that he had a wealthy family made him a target.

It was only a few days into my sentence when I had my first visit from the British embassy. I was taken over to the main gate and Nigel, one of the managers from the embassy in Nairobi, was waiting for me with money, soap and toilet roll.

Jill, his understudy, was with him and he stood holding a copy of the *Daily Nation* in one hand and told me I'd made the headlines. He showed me the front page and a close up shot of me in court looking sorry for myself.

"Let's hope the English papers don't get hold of this," he said.

I did wonder what all the fuss was about. A year in prison – so what? But as I found out during my time there, not many foreigners went to prison in Africa – they paid the bribe, so a white British sixty-year old sentenced to serve time in an African prison was a novelty and certainly newsworthy. The visits from the embassy were always supervised every four weeks and it was always Jill who took over from Nigel; she was in her late fifties and she always came with a younger trainee. She'd lived here for the past four years with her Kenyan boyfriend. The meeting would last about ten minutes with a guard standing, watching and listening. They used to leave money in the office for my basic needs like soap and toothpaste, toilet paper. The guards loved my visits more than I did – my money was their money. The kitty they held for me was for basic rations and when I needed certain things I'd send messages over to the office to different people to try and use some of it but I wouldn't hear back from them for weeks and would in the end have to borrow from someone else.

The main idea of Camp David was that it was used as a selection centre or a base for the new intakes so the officers could assess where they went: The Farm, Mainstream or Segregation.

At the end of the week we had to go over to the main office for the process to take place. The Second Officer in Charge sat at a desk with another guard stood behind him, holding a baton. We all filed in, straight onto our haunches and immediately the Officer in Charge shouted, "You there, get down." No one dared to flinch. The guard acting on his behalf swept around the desk in one swift move, baton drawn, jabbing this bloke's face with it. "Stand up." He did this slowly, confused, looking back at the officer not sure what to do. His first reaction was to raise his elbows to shield his face from the baton which was now whacking him.

"Now get down," the poor bloke was bewildered at first but then realised his mistake and crouched closer to the floor. The officer sat upright while he read from some paper in front of him, then with authority in his voice he spoke again. He called names out and referred back to his sheet. "You... Farm," pointing, then referring back to the paper. The information he was reading was everyone's crimes. If he came across a crime he didn't like, he'd give the nod and that person was beaten, others waiting would shake in fear of being next.

He came to me. "You – Segregation." Segregation, I was told, was the place rapists and robbers and runners (repeat escapees) were kept, away from the Mainstream for the sake of their own and others' safety.

To them I was an old, and at that time, poorly and weak small time drug smuggler – a threat to no one. So why was I put there? Was it for my own safety? If it was then why was I sharing a block with robbers and rapists. I couldn't suss that one out straight away but as time went on I understood why, and it wasn't for my own safety.

30. Segregation

The officer could see I was in no fit state for manual labour so he did me a favour there. I worked on a farm back in the seventies so working the land did appeal to me but I was younger and fitter back then. It would've slaughtered me now, especially on this farm. It was strange because it wasn't that long ago that I was cracking rocks, setting the standards in that quarry, and I realised then how traumatic remand and the last few months had been. That experience traumatised me, stripping my body of muscle and strength which had been my trademark throughout my working life.

I wouldn't have lasted very long on that farm, that's for sure. I got to know very quickly from the lads returning from there how hard it was. They treated the animals better. They rationed their food and worked them until it was dark. Solid graft and random beatings, that was farm work.

The guards have to make sure the prisoners working on the farm didn't smuggle anything back into the prison; cigarettes, drugs or even a sharp weapon so they had this routine inspection.

On their return to the prison they would all be gathered together, counted and then ordered to strip naked and single file hop like frogs across the compound. When I first saw this I thought it was a Monty Python sketch. It was bizarre. All eyes were on the hoppers as they made their way back to the cells, making sure nothing fell out of their ass. Now that's attention to detail.

Like most situations there, money dictated and the staff were always too happy to take a bribe. The few who came from wealthy families paid the Officer in Charge a monthly wage for them to get an easier time on the farm with a few perks like better food, but for the majority, it was long hours of hard and sometimes torturous graft.

163

Even so, most of the people in Camp David were desperate to work on the farm and the ones picked with me to go to Segregation were disappointed. I spoke to one bloke who was always in and out of prison; he loved working on the farm.

"Yeh, it's hard work and you get beaten, but hey, all this is outside in fields, it feels like you're not a prisoner – that's why everyone wants to work on the farm." Segregation, he explained, is a lonely place. You're locked up most of the day and the only exercise is that small yard. I could see his point. His face changed and his expression livened as he explained about the scenery and the animals that moved across it as you work in the open fields.

Segregation was an unmanned barrier away from Mainstream prison and my block was a rectangular concrete building with seventeen cells serviced by a gated corridor which ran the length of the building. The standpipe on one side of a low partition was for us to wash ourselves – when they felt like turning the water on, and a chained bucket for a toilet, which rarely got emptied, was on the other. A gate at the opposite end led to a small courtyard.

The first was the punishment cell and the second was to keep sex offenders, the mentally challenged and any other oddballs away.

I wasn't expecting the food to be any different from remand or Camp David and it wasn't but it always seemed to be late by an hour or even two.

On the other side of the high wall was Maximum Kamiti for offenders of crimes (five-year sentences minimum).

They kept getting power cuts so we had to cook their food and take it in for them and that's why there were the delays. Next door was all electric whereas we cooked using wood for fuel. The solution would be for them to use wood like us but taking wood into a place like that, they would end up killing the guards with it. So we had to wait.

Normally the food was brought over by an askari or kitchen staff, so to see a sergeant taking time out to do this job was very unusual and as soon as I saw him I knew this meal was going to be expensive.

It was common knowledge that I had money at the office and it was "mzungu" most of the time, but when they wanted something, it got all formal.

"Mr Johnson, I need to speak." Then he started whispering, "Can I take a hundred shillings? My wife is ill…" and before he rattled on about how ill she was I just cut him short. Yep, no problem. I knew all the excuses and the real reason for the money. They had the purse strings to my money and I suppose I could have said no but I would be refusing desperate people and it's these desperate people who are in charge of me, so my answer was always yes. I saw the same officer the following day – he more or less blanked me, no greeting or acknowledgement. I moved to the bars and could smell the booze as he passed by. Money well spent, I thought.

Now and again they would spike the evening meal, not sure how or what they used but out of the blue we'd all have the shits. The next day the stench and mess around us was unbearable, it was vile. We then waited to slop out, and when they did eventually open the gate we'd get to the standpipe with our bucket, turn it on and guess what? No water. When the askari did show up they would say, "Right, only two of you are allowed out, take the buckets and go over to the kitchen and get the water." The kitchen is less than fifty yards away and the boys would fight to go over there because it gave them a chance to wash and smoke a cigarette.

I used to wake up very early in the morning, lie there and listen to distant sounds. Women screaming over the wall where the askaris lived and dogs always barking. The dogs they kept were mainly Alsatians, lean, mean-looking things always tied up and stressed out with the heat.

Most mornings at about seven, I'd hear the gates open and two askaris would come in - the one who had been on duty all night and a higher ranking officer. We'd all stand up and be counted, then in their own time and depending on the morning shift and what mood they were in, the doors would open with a stampede to the toilets to empty buckets. This wasn't always the case of course, and if we had a bad one he'd keep us waiting for the exercise yard, and our breakfast.

This was the first check of the day and another four or five followed later. A giant gong hung in the middle of the compound which they hit with a drumstick; a 'bong' sound vibrated around the prison and no matter where you were you had to drop to your haunches and wait. The askari would come in through the gate with pen and paper, counting and writing as he walked and you would have to wait till everyone in the whole compound and inside the prison was counted. The sun at midday was unbearable so if you happened to be outside and the count started, you had no time to move into the shade. Sometimes I'd be out there for forty-five minutes and then they would shout 'miscount' and start all over again.

31. Cigarettes and Raids

Cigarettes were banned in the prison, and if you were caught smoking you were beaten, so you had to find a place away from them to smoke. It wasn't always the guards who were the problem, a crafty secret fag moment could be gate-crashed by a crowd of inmates surrounding me, all wanting a smoke. The no smoking rule didn't stop the guards from selling them; they went outside and bought the cheapest, strongest ones they could find, bring them in and sell to the lucky ones with money for double the mark-up price.

Conveniently, and like they had planned it the day before, the next day, the guards would charge in and raid our cells and take all the cigarettes back again and over the next few days we had no choice; if we wanted to smoke then we'd have to buy them back again and so the scam went on.

At night-time all the doors were locked and nobody could open them. You couldn't even get into the prison because the person with the keys went home into the village, which was out of the compound and the prison couldn't be opened until he came back the following day. So the guards had already worked out that the best time to hit us and to find out what we had was first thing in the morning when we were unable to move it or hide it from our cell.

Twenty or thirty of them piled in, unlocked the doors at seven, ordering us to crouch down while they went charging around the cells ripping and tossing everything around, looking for money or fags.

When they'd finished they went out into the yard and everyone would come out slowly, in single file so you couldn't pass anything to anybody. Then they'd search you. If they found something they'd normally give you a slap or a clout with a stick. Half the time they didn't even bother searching me, they just ordered me back in.

Every cell had a Boy in Charge; a prisoner in charge of the others, a kind of go-between or a Mr Fix It character for the guard. Mine was John; he had no authority, he was just there so the guards could find out things about us. He never had visitors and always seemed to have cigarettes (and one for me) which was good. Towards the end of my sentence I asked him, "Look, I know the ropes here now and I get the odd bit of money sent through, but I always run out of fags but you always seem to 'ave 'em."

He smiled. "I have a way but I can't tell you."

One day, a tall inmate came over from another block and asked where John was, I told him he was with the doctor. Now was my chance to ask.

"Oh, I've got some cigarettes for him," he told me.

"What's that for then?"

He looking uneasy then he leaned in closer and told me.

"Well, I can only come over here when a certain guard is on your gate to let me in and I've got to ask permission from your friend to go in number seventeen and fuck the young boy there." I wished I'd never asked.

I also reminded myself about being a British subject in the prison of a Commonwealth country with monthly embassy visits. I was lucky I had rights that most in there didn't have and I played on that to survive. I was never cocky but it did give me strength in mind and a measure of confidence that made the guards leave me alone. I had a connection with the outside and knew I could influence change to them and their lives.

The outside yard we exercised in was enclosed by a fifteen-foot wall topped with rolls of barbed wire, and this was where we exercised. It was roughly twenty-feet square and I soon got fed up with walking in circles, so I occupied my mind in other ways. Like the alphabet game again.

I turned my back and got the lads to write the alphabet in the dust with the stick, and each letter's corresponding number; they would then shout out a random number or letter and I would shout the answer. The only rule was, I couldn't take any longer than a second to answer and they took turns testing me and I got each one right. The next day, a bloke ran up to me, "Mr Johnson, what's 17?"

A second later I said, "Q."

"I told you, didn't I?" he said to his mate as they walked away.

I also challenged them to walking races across the yard.

"Come on, I will beat anyone over a short distance." They lined up and had a go.

Now these lads were obviously younger, stronger and fitter than me but over a short distance I was confident. I discovered this talent when I played rugby as a kid; no one could beat me.

I got one of them to judge from a side-on stance to make sure they were walking and not running. To keep up with me they ended running and got disqualified. I couldn't beat them running but fast walking they didn't stand a chance.

I noticed when the others exercised they never looked up to the sky; obviously they were used to their own wildlife but I never got tired of looking up and seeing different things.

The weather gets cooler in July and August, and I wondered how this was possible when the sun burns behind the clouds anyway, but I watched the sky during these months and understood why. A layer of cloud would come across and cover the first one and then another would do the same. In the end, the sky would have three layers of cloud and that kept the temperature down to about twenty-one degrees in the daytime and about eleven or twelve degrees at night, and all the time I was there it rained for just one day and that was just a light drizzle.

When the rainy season starts, so do the frogs, thousands of them and the noise they made was deafening. After about ten minutes they'd all stop and we'd have complete silence and then they'd start again – this went on all night. It drove me bloody crackers.

Once I walked out and saw a flock of kites hovering and swooping down to a tree over the other side of the wall. I found a spot in the yard where I could see what was happening. The tree was full of brightly coloured weaver birds flitting, fussing around their nests and these kites were busy attacking them. I liked the way the kites hung in the air, swooping down but I felt sorry for these weaver birds and straight away took their side. I collected small stones in amongst the dust and started throwing them at the kites. I kept throwing until my arm ached, but the kites were relentless; they kept prodding the nests.

"Mr Johnson, what are doing?"

"Well, I'm trying to save the weaver birds."

"Mr Johnson, the kites will win."

"I know but I gotta try, man."

He laughed. "I know but you're wasting your time."

Another lad had turned up with some string in a type of lasso and I asked him what it was for.

He had a ball of ugali stuck in the loop, took it to the corner of the yard and waited for a bird. When it landed and took the bait he pulled it but missed and the bird flew away, but an hour later he caught one, not sure what it was but it had amazing vivid colours.

"What you going do with that now?"

"I'll let him go. Just a bit of fun."

There were a few prisoners who were treated differently from the rest. Big-built guys who seemed to have more privileges than anyone else. When we were all locked up we could see them outside their cell laughing and joking with the guards. Later, I found out these guys were the minders. In certain situations they would do the guards' dirty work like carry out tortures and beatings.

The prison was full of all different tribes, the largest tribe in Kenya is the Kikuyu. I did notice one guy there who was from one of the lesser tribes, not sure which one, but the new guard that came on duty one night got very excited when he heard his voice. The guard came up to the bars in the door and they were both talking for ten minutes in their own language. Every time that guard came on duty that boy was favoured and it worked the other way as well, as the unpopular tribes were given a harder time.

There was another building about twenty metres away from us; the same type of building, cell blocks and a yard. I could see the guys walking around in the small dusty yard the same as us there, waiting to go to court. They were a mixed race group; Indians, Pakistanis and darker-skinned people.

We had one bloke from Pakistan with us; I noticed the Africans accepted him but were ready to criticise him at any time. Most of the businesses over there are run by Indians and Pakistanis; they seem to have a knack of making money and this causes a bit of tension between the communities. An Indian bloke used to bring our food over; he would always talk to me, he spoke very good English.

"They just caught me with a cigarette and beat me," he said, lifting his shirt and showing me his back, which was blackened with bruises.

32. Denied, Denied, Denied

Like at school, you had good and bad teachers, here was no different, albeit the bad ones outweighed the good ones. The Personnel Officer's job was the welfare of the prisoners and he was mainly office-based but was a total pushover. Sometimes he would cover shifts that took him away from his desk and the boys looked forward to this.

In the mornings they used to look down towards the gate straining their necks before the doors opened to see who was on duty. One morning, I could hear them all chatting and sounding happy as they spotted the meek and mild-mannered Personnel Officer covering for sickness.

His job was very much about needing to be seen doing something, and like the hotel manager who I mimicked years ago doing his inspection around the hotel pool, this bloke made his visit official looking with a clipboard and pen.

All he did was go around and ask prisoners if they had any requests or if they wanted an appointment with the Officer in Charge. Now there's an unwritten rule with new intakes; when the Personnel Officer comes around, no one tells you that it's a complete waste of time.

The first time I met him the boys started smoking and acting far more casual in front of him than with any other officer and all they got from him was, "Oi, you're not supposed to smoke, you know."

The boys put in their requests just to encourage me to do the same and left me thinking I was getting coffee and tea and a newspaper; that was enough to start with, I didn't want to take the piss.

He came back later to see me with his clipboard and told me everything I had requested had been denied; he showed me as he crossed out each item on the list. Denied, denied, denied. No explanation, he just turned on his heels and marched away and the boys behind burst out laughing. The Boy in Charge explained, "When you see him again it's good news; you can do a lot more things with him on duty but if he asks you if you have any requests, don't bother because everything is denied, denied, denied."

It was the Administration Office but we all called it 'the office'. It was a place to fear and was designed with two uses in mind; I saw the look on prisoners' faces when their names were called to go there.

It was a long building with six or seven separate rooms and each one had metal grilles on the door. The large open area seemed a complete waste of space as all the rooms of it were small in size. The room at the end was used to keep everybody's clothes when they first arrived and was full of dust.

If you had money to collect from this place or you had favours to give or visitors to see, then it was fine. If not, then it was bad news because the only other reason you came here was for a brutal inhumane punishment. Officers gathered and watched on as prisoners were lined up naked and shackled to the metal grille windows. Most sentences carried an additional lashing or two and even after their quota, prisoners could still be called over at any time and led to believe they were going to be lashed, only to find out that it wasn't the case. The guards enjoyed a bit of mental torture and, depending on the mood of the Officer in Charge, they just got a slap across the face, or a favourite trick was making them lie on the floor face down and then whack them with a stick or chain.

Every Thursday at ten or eleven in the morning, the same music would play loud enough to drown out the noise as the gates opened and about a dozen, naked waiting prisoners would go into the office. A salt water gauze was placed across their buttocks to stop the bleeding and a bloke limbered up with the stick in front of the guards, including the Officer in Charge, who paid an extra fifty pence (a day's wages) if he did a good job. The stick used was the meanest, most wicked-looking thing, perfectly tapered and shaped; purpose-built for the job, and he was allowed to bring his arm back as far as he liked for maximum impact. Once inside, they cranked the music up to drown out the echo of noise from the building and every week the same single thought went through my head. This is barbaric – into a new Millennium and they still do this.

Once I turned away from watching them go in and clocked my surroundings, the people in the room and questioned the reality of where I was. Was I dreaming it? How could I be here? Was it real? I walked out into the yard and circled the dust, looking up to the clouds, looking over at the weaver birds and watching the kites.

"Mzungu. Is there a word called 'sod'?" I spun round; they were playing Scrabble.

"Yeh," I answered and went back into my trance of deep thought.

They quite often used me as ref for games, qualifying English they were making up.

The other bloke asked me what it was.

"You can have a sod of earth, it's the lump of soil that connects to the roots of grass."

"See? He knows, he's a white man," the bloke said, counting up the numbers on his word. I left them to it and stood on my own, reflecting on my situation. This is no dream. I am really here.

I started walking, circling again and a large flying insect passed me with long spindly legs. I stopped, and noticed something in its mouth as it made its way up the wall and into the eaves of the roof where it was building a clay nest. Not sure what it was called but I know it had a bad sting, it had me a few times. It was going to and fro. I wanted to see how intelligent this thing was so I reached up and took a piece of clay away from the nest and watched its reaction. It returned with more clay and straight away spotted the big hole in his nest, and with that, started to buzz around like mad. One of the boys came out and asked me what I was doing.

"I'm only testing it."

"It will test you in a minute if it stings you." Luckily the insect had a short memory and carried on building its clay house.

At the start of my sentence I used to fantasise about food like hamburger and chips drenched in salt and vinegar. Then I reached a point when all these desires went; I just stopped thinking about them and I think this was the turning point of my sentence. I couldn't from that time onwards remember having a boring day and yet I was where I was. Something really did happen to me in prison.

33. Body Lice and Cadbury's

One of the men in my cell was a hard man, big and strong, in his twenties, and had been caught for a violent robbery in Nairobi.

One Thursday his name was called and they took him to the doctor, like they did with everyone, to see if he was fit enough for punishment. Then they took him to the office. He came back an hour later and he never spoke that day, or the next one after – in fact, everyone was frightened to speak to him; they feared him, he was like a time bomb ticking quietly away and they were expecting him to explode at any point. I couldn't stand the atmosphere any longer so I chanced it.

"Come on, drop your trousers." I could see and feel everyone's shock as I said the words. This giant man had been standing for the best part of two days just glared at me.

"Come on, let's see what those bastards have done to you." He didn't move straight away which did concern me. He moved his arm down to unfasten the button on his trousers, dropping them to the floor and turned around. One stroke, that's all, had made a welt, a groove so deep I could hide my thumbnail, and after two days it still wept like it had just been done. It sliced into his thick Kenyan skin like butter and looked like a tyre mark, like someone had driven over him. They're only allowed to give one stroke at any one time so if you were sentenced with three strokes then you woke every following Thursday fearing the worst for a repeat performance at the office. A stroke at my age and in my health ... I don't think I would have survived the trauma of that experience – thankfully I never had to.

The next problem we had to contend with, apart from the guards, were 'Chawa'. Sharing a small space in that heat was the perfect breeding ground for them. Chawa were body lice and I would wake up and see them crawling across my chest, some as chunky as my nail. Powder is all that was needed to stop them but the officers didn't want to know I guess. To them it was all part of our punishment. Every day after breakfast the lads would race outside to pick the sunniest spot on the barbed fence to hang their blankets. The heat from the sun would draw them out and the boys stood poised ready to squeeze them with their thumbs. That was the only way we could control them. We all took turns in cleaning our cell, but without hot water, bleach or disinfectant, it wasn't easy keeping the bugs away. Starting at one end, two lads would hold a corner of a wet blanket, draping it and would at the same time run backwards mopping the floor with other end. They nearly knocked me out once. Two lads shot back and didn't see me behind them and when I saw them I wasn't quick enough to move out of the way and they sent me flying.

Whenever an askari came on duty, one of the lads stood by with a bucket in case he wanted to sit down.

One sergeant in particular would walk around the prison and when he was in a good mood he used to come over to our place in Segregation to see us. He used to come out into the yard, take his seat on an upside down bucket and the lads, about half a dozen, flocked around him, sat on the ground, looking up like kids listening to his stories. One day sarge was on his bucket telling his stories as usual while I was walking in circles, still throwing the odd stone at those bloody kites, and I could more or less get the gist of what they were saying.

"Right, watch the mzungu now, watch what he does," he said to them.

"Mzungu," he yelled.

"Yes Sir."

"You see what I mean?" he was using me as an example for good manners.

"He responded quickly, obediently and did that all in one movement and called me 'Sir'. That's the British for you, they've got manners, why can't you be more like him?"

Most of the inmates were illiterate, had never been to school, some never had parents to teach them social skills and good manners, and no money or food, so I could see why they were in and out of prison – crime was their survival and who could blame them?

My only connection with the outside world was my once a month visit with Jill from the embassy. No tv or phones, but they allowed you to write letters. However, I did find that a complete waste of time because they opened the letters before they left prison and if anything was said that they didn't agree with, your letter was destroyed. You can write a nice letter and ask for money – they liked that and when it came back, they took the lot. If you had post you had to go to Administration and you would have to open it in front of the guard and any money would be handed over. I was called over a few times for letters from my sister, and one time I had a package from her. A guard and the Officer in Charge were waiting for me in the office. The officer greeted me and produced a rectangle shape, wrapped in brown paper. He turned it over in his hand as he talked, and a section of wrapping paper was missing. I looked, trying to guess what it was and saw a flash of purple shiny wrapping, and I instantly recognised my favourite chocolate. He let me unwrap it and I held it, turning the kilo slab of Cadbury's milk chocolate in my hands.

I'd been surviving on watered milk, potatoes, shoe leather meat and gruel for the last eight months. No coffee, no tea and no sugar. This was going to be heaven. Still holding it, my dry mouth was now salivating at the thought of me snapping this into chunks, melting it into a sweet, creamy goo. I was ready to scoff the lot.

"You can't have it."

"Why not?" He didn't answer straight away. "Why not?"

"It could be poison," he said, grim-faced, shaking his head.

"I'll take that chance." My answer was only a verbal disclaimer but I was happy to sign as well.

"No, we can't let you take that chance."

"But I want to take that chance."

No was their final answer. Apparently they have a duty of care, a responsibility for me. They let me starve in remand, ignoring my reasons for not eating their food – that was ok but when chocolate arrived for me, they suddenly care that it could poison me. My guess was that the officers had a treat that night.

The only time I got lucky with an edible gift was when Jill from the embassy brought me some wedding cake. She'd just got married in Nairobi to a local guy and turned up on her monthly visit with a slab of cake. We sat down together and chatted under supervision as usual as she produced this box. The guard looked at me as I took it. No, not this time, I thought. I opened it and broke it up with my fingers and ate the lot. The smell and taste, the moist richness, brandy and sugar was intoxicating. I felt giddy afterwards, a real sugar rush, but it was worth it.

On the next embassy visit I asked Jill for a decent pair of flip flops. The ones I was given were rough cuts of rubber that shredded my feet, making them sore. When Jill arrived, I requested this in front of the Officer in Charge and permission was granted. I saw the askari who gave me the flip flops and eight cigarettes for trading in my old ones, so that was a good bit of business.

34. Toe Nail Man

Razor blades were officially banned but there was one bloke who was allowed to have one, and we all trusted him with one.

He was an expert with a razor blade and used to cut my toe-nails with it. I'd give him a cigarette or fifty bob if I had it. He had a few customers on his round and had a good thing going, making a few bob here and there, and he became known as the Toenail Man. One day, he was ordered out of Segregation; no one knew why, the guards were mean and just wanted to end his little business. The next day, we all heard someone on the main prison roof, ranting, going berserk, shouting, screaming; he was naked and from a distance he looked like he'd covered himself in mud but we found out it was his own shit. He covered himself in his own shit as some sort of dirty protest, and in the end, they brought him down, knocked him around a bit with their sticks and then took him to the nearest tap and hosed him down. Once clean they beat him again and next day he was back with us smiling, cutting nails again. Business as usual.

Once a month, another bloke came in and cut our hair. If it wasn't kept short we'd all end up with lice and other nasties.

One of the inmates wasn't the full ticket and had a huge boil on his neck and I could see he was in a lot of pain. I went across to these lads and said, "Right, this man is suffering. The doctor isn't going to do anything so we need to help."

"We're all suffering, we haven't had a fag all day," one of the others piped up, not at all sympathetic.

"I will get you a cigarette to share if you help me," I said. So the four of us held him down and squeezed open this boil; he shouted and screamed and then we realised we didn't have any toilet paper, which was difficult to get hold of at the best of times, but another fag got some and we used it to soak up the pus. Five minutes later, the lads were sharing their fag and Boil Man was boil-less and in less pain, so it all ended well.

Once a week, it was doctor's day and this caused a hell of a fuss. Everyone wanted to see the doctor. The officer would unlock the doors and announce the arrival of the doctor. On hearing the word 'doctor' they raced from their cells to form a line up in the corridor, getting into position, down on their haunches, they waited for the Officer in Charge. Starting at one end he went down the line choosing those he thought were sick enough to see the doctor. In turn, he'd face each one and tell them, and those not looking or acting sick enough, he would push over using the flat of his foot. "You're not sick, you and you, not sick," and so on, bowling them over with his foot like skittles. If it was Chui, not many were picked and sometimes no one saw him. "You, you, you, you, you, you, and you – you're not sick, back to your cells."

I was given the job at the chalkboard and the askari would shout, "Right, I'm taking eight over," and that was my cue to mark the board with the number eight and when they came back I stood ready with chalk in my hand.

"Right, eight back," and I'd mark the board again.

I went once, took a walk over to the compound where the doctor was. It had planted borders with vibrant coloured flowers, and it was nice to see instead of the normal concrete outlook. I could see why everyone wanted to see the doctor. People mooched around, casually chatting and were free to smoke. I found a cigarette from someone and stood in the shade and watched the place; it seemed peaceful and not part of the prison.

The same reaction happened for Library day.

"Right, line up for the library," and they instantly bolted down on their haunches, walking the line, knocking them all over. "You can't, you can't, you can't go...You! You can't even fucking read."

"I look at the pictures," was his response. I used to go over for a cigarette now and again just to see what the craic was and was met at the door and given a tatty book or a magazine to read. You didn't get a choice, it was whatever he handed you. I went three or four times and he gave me the same fucking book. I read the only newspaper word for word and it was over two years old so it wasn't even news.

Every time I went to the library the same bloke was there; as soon as he saw me he would spring off his seat and rush up to me greet me using big words from the Thesaurus he carried around with him and the conversation would go something like this;

"Good afternoon, Mr Johnson, how are you this fine day?"

"Fucking marvellous, how's you?"

"Oh, I feel blithesome today," he said. I didn't have a clue what he was on about. He referred back to his book and told me what he meant. "Cheery."

Then say that, or that you're fine, or if you really are, then say you're happy or great.

I would have the same chat with him over and over. I explained that most people didn't use words like that in England and advised him to keep it simple. He never did listen and when we met he'd have a new big word for me.

He was from Nairobi and he was serving three years for a robbery and knew Kamiti very well from two other visits. I started asking him questions about release, what happens and that. The last time he was at the prison they released him with enough money to get him half way home on the bus so he had to walk the rest of the way, which he said was about twenty miles. Not enough to get home, no money to live on or feed his family so he'd be back up to no good again and every time this happened he went back to prison, and his family suffered even more without their breadwinner.

"I tell you what, when I get home I'm going to send you some money. They will keep it for when you leave, for your last day." The more I spoke the more his expression changed to disbelief.

"That's not possible. They will never give me money."

"I have a plan! You wait and see."

"You leave soon and you're going to remember next year when I leave and you're going to send me some money?"

"Yeh."

He shook his head again. "Even if you do they will keep the money."

"You'll see, I have a plan."

His release date was just before Easter the following year. My plan was to send a letter to the First Officer in charge with forty pounds, twenty for the First Officer in Charge and a separate envelope with the other twenty for Jacob. My letter would instruct the officer to buy sweets for the children as they come out of church on Easter Sunday and any change left over to be spent between the officers. I also sent a separate letter to the church telling them I would be sending the money so they would be expecting their donation. I enclosed a letter to Jacob and post-scripted it with the following statement. 'Don't worry, I know your handwriting so I will know it's really you.' I did this just in case someone else started contacting me pretending to be Jacob. The fact was, if he did reply I'd have no problem recognising him by his choice of words and it was a way of fending off the scammers. It was a long shot but I knew if the letter was sent to the top man and the church were informed, then Jacob stood a good chance of getting his money. It was worth a go.

One of the longest serving prisoners saved a bit of money and installed his own radio, wiring the corridor so we could all hear it. This was, we all thought at the time, a great idea but all it ended up doing was putting another bullet in their gun because now they could turn it on any time they wanted. They put on music the boys loved such as Reggae and as soon they heard Bob Marley or anything similar they went wild, dancing around the place. The guards, sensing they were having too much fun, would leave the dial between stations on full volume, the crackling echoing throughout the building drove us mad for hours. Sunday evenings were something to look forward when the radio blasted out religious programs. I ended up sitting with my hands over my ears waiting for it to end. You never knew when it would come on again; there were sometimes weeks of silence and then full blast again.

35. 9/11 and Christmas

"Ok everyone, out – quick!" It wasn't meal or a break time so I wondered what all the fuss was about. I was told not to go but the others were ordered out. The Boy in Charge persuaded the askari to let me join in and he agreed so I walked out to join the others.

Flying ants bigger than I've ever seen before swarmed around, covering the ground.

"Come on then, move it, before the birds get them." Not sure what I was doing at first but I could see a plastic container they were filling so I did the same.

During the night the wings drop off and if you're not quick enough, they disappear underground or the birds will have them. That's what the call up was for – breakfast of flying ants.

The guards used to fry them alive in coconut oil, apparently it's high in protein and makes a tasty treat, but I didn't fancy finding out. So we were all out there picking these ants off the floor and we ended up filling half of a four-litre plastic container. I found out afterwards that the askari got a bollocking from the sergeant. The mzungu shouldn't have gone out there. I'm not sure why, but when they all went out the next night to do it all again, I wasn't allowed.

I got used to seeing the same old faces doing the same old thing so it was nice when we got new inmates. Six new prisoners came in one day and I found out they were serving soldiers in the Kenyan Army. They got six weeks in Kamiti for stealing from the pay office. I got talking, joking and laughing with them. The sergeant in charge of them all wanted to know all about me, so I told him my story.

After a few days, they were telling me how tough the prison was and how tough the Army is, and like the prisons over there, it's like the British Army was in the fifties, very strict and sometimes brutal, but he said he'd never experienced anything like Kamiti.

"How long have you got left here?" he asked me.

"Four weekends to go," I said, keeping a straight face.

The Boy in Charge piped up. "Don't listen to him. He's got seven months to go yet."

"Seven months! I've only been here three weeks and it feels like three months. This place is nightmare, a complete nightmare."

I was in my cell when the duty askari came especially to tell me something."

"Hey, your lot are getting bombed." At the time I didn't have a clue what he was on about, I didn't even question what he was saying, but he was referring to 9/11. Strange to think I was where I was when that happened.

My first and hopefully my last Christmas in Kamiti.

I was only sentenced for a year but you never know with Kenya – anything can happen. "Mr Johnson, we've made a mistake, your sentence should have been three years," was a recurring nightmare in my head.

There was no way of knowing that we were ten days from Christmas. The place looked exactly the same as any other time, except the Personnel Officer threw some festive cheer when doing the rounds with his Christmas requests. I knew all about the Personnel Officer and ignored him while he asked the others what they wanted for Christmas dinner. Most of them took no notice but the few new ones answered; turkey, pork, mash, carrots, roast potatoes, pudding, custard... and so the list went on. He came back ten minutes later. "Denied, denied, denied, denied..."

"What we gunna have then?" said one chap.

"The same as you've had the last three hundred and sixty-four days."

Every once in a while the Government gave prisons the authority to pardon and allow prisoners to go free. It happened once when I was there and they make it a real pomp and ceremony occasion.

The main compound was transformed for the day with a podium, flowers and bunting arranged and we were all ordered to line up outside to squat. The officers stood up in full uniform and we all waited for the Officer in Charge to appear and take his position on the podium.

A long speech in Swahili was interrupted as we all looked up to see jets screaming overhead to mark the occasion. He droned on for another twenty minutes and then he was handed the book and the crazy game show began. He paused before each name for dramatic effect, looking down at us with everyone staring back, waiting for his lips to move.

His name was announced and he went wild; I'll never forget his reaction. He screamed and started running both hands above his hands waving, beaming his smile back to encourage us all to clap and cheer.

The guards marked out the route towards the main entrance and this bloke was so overcome with the emotion of being picked he ran straight into the line of guards who reacted by beating him back on course with their sticks. He didn't seem to mind; he was a free man and kept waving and cheering back at the crowd.

I got talking to someone else who had been in and out of Kamiti all his life and who explained, reliving his own pardon experience. Once out of sight from the crowd and podium a gang of askaris waited so they could beat him. "I never really felt the pain," he said. "I laughed the whole time and they got fed up beating me in the end."

The askari next to me said, "He'll soon be back, he won't survive out there."

The end of my sentence approached, and the last two days dragged so slowly it was mind numbing. Up until then I had taken every day as it came and each one offered me something different. My time served in prison was challenging, frustrating and sometimes painful, but never boring.

I was lucky that as a British citizen, I had support from the embassy, I was never beaten and the only time was a rap over the knuckles in the courtyard but that was hardly a beating. Apart from the extra food in remand, I was treated the same as the others but I did play the system a bit.

My age, and the fact I was the only white man serving time in a black man's prison, frightened the shit out of me to start with but as time progressed, my body, mind and confidence grew stronger and I realised they feared me as much as I feared them.

I realised that they didn't want me in prison to start with, that's why they put me in Segregation with rapists and robbers – not, because like them I was a danger to the mainstream, but it was to keep me away from their prison and the way they saw fit to run it. They did their best to hide things but I saw and heard too much. Casting my mind back to the airport, I had no money but I got the feeling fifty quid would have sorted it – they were desperate people but they also didn't want the hassle of dealing with a foreigner and gave me plenty of chances to ask friends or family, but I didn't. I punished myself for not asking for help, as I said before, it was my mess.

36. Release

The day before I was released, they called me over to the laundry. The clothes I arrived in were bagged up, stored on racks. I had this vision that the place would be a pokey, stifling hot room tucked away somewhere in the prison but I was surprised when I got there.

It was open air, surrounded by a high wall, planted flowers and the staff working there seemed relaxed and easy going. Everything was washed by hand and hung up to dry, and the chap there gave me my shirt and told me my trousers would be ready the next day with a crease.

The next day, I woke early and lay wide awake for two hours before the askari opened the gate and shouted my name. I couldn't wait to get out, free to taste tea or coffee and smoke as and when I wanted to. To taste the food I knew was out there, food I'd been denied. I was already changed and ready and I said my goodbyes, taking a quick glance around before I left – I ain't gonna miss this place, I thought, that's for certain.

I asked the guard if the Boy in Charge could come over to the gate with me. When we all got there my mate realised he had the wrong top on but it was too late, they ordered him to lie flat on the floor on his stomach; we both knew what was coming. His pitiful look up at me said it all.

Interrupting the sergeant doing his paperwork, I whispered, pleading to show this bloke some mercy. He agreed, ordering the guard to take him back to Segregation. He gave me a thumbs up and a big smile as he left. Not beaten out front, probably beaten inside, but he seemed happy.

My clothes were all laid out and the sergeant disappeared, leaving me alone with just one askari, so I perched on the corner of the table and waited for the embassy officials to arrive.

"Oi, get off there, who do you think you are?" said the guard. It was my last day and I wondered what his problem was. Money. My money. He obviously dipped out of my fund and sounded bitter in his tone; it wasn't for the benefit of anyone, just aimed at me so that was the only reason I could think of.

This place was normally quite busy; four or five people at any time but it was virtually empty. I was being released and was expecting the embassy to come in so maybe it was arranged like this.

I stood on my own in the doorway for over an hour just waiting, looking around, studying the room in more detail and I saw something that made me laugh.

A notice stated the word 'Concession: As of today prisoners are allowed to wear underpants.' I read it and repeated it aloud. "You are now allowed to wear underpants?" I turned to the guard to question the new rule.

"Underpants, don't you know?" said the guard, with even more attitude.

"Yeh, I know what underpants are but why would we wear them in here? They would just fill up with body lice, with Chawa." Some concession that was.

I paced the office floor, thinking they'd forgotten me, or that there was some sort of mistake.

Two hours later, Nigel and Jill arrived and apologised. We didn't have time to pick up my passport which was in the main port on the other side of the city so we had to move fast.

When it was time, another askari came across and took me to the main gate and within the distance between the gate and the car stood another askari, it was clear he was waiting to speak to me. He was a good one who I'd trusted throughout my sentence with money but he looked anxious, I could tell he had something to tell me.

"Mr Johnson, I'm very sorry about this money, my children have been sick, been out of work…"

About six months earlier, Ted had sent me some money for

my release and I was just about to find out most of it had been taken by the guards, including him, but he was the only one to admit and apologise and that said a lot about him.

"Look, don't fucking worry, man. That's all in the past, son. I'm free, I'm out from here. This is a good day. The best day of my life."

The last time I'd seen Nigel was in remand, showing me my photo on the front page. I remembered him and what he said back then.

"When you get out of here, we'll take you to our favourite eating place. It's our treat, choose anything you like." I've got twelve months to make my choice, I thought, but in the meantime I'll have the maize and cabbage off the specials. It was tradition for them to take the 'releases' out for a meal.

The smell of the restaurant rushed up my nose and into my mouth as the door opened – it was overwhelming. It had been sixteen months of the same severe diet; now this was going to be a treat or a shock to the system. I did wonder how my body would cope with the richness of the food but I was willing to give it a go and my long awaited fantasy of burger and chips was just about to become a reality.

Sounds silly, but I'd actually forgotten what burger and chips actually tasted like. My senses had been dulled down by the same bland food so I was ready for this. Now working overtime, I could smell warm doughy bread mixed in with the scent of the waitress pouring my coffee, which funnelled up my nose. Beef burger and chips would never taste the same again. "It's been a long time."

As I ripped open a sugar sachet from the condiments and poured it into my mouth, that wedding cake moment returned.

I drenched my chips with salt and vinegar, and took hold of my burger in both hands and tore into it. Grease squelched out of the meat, lacing my mouth and lubricating my throat with every bite. It was bloody heaven. We couldn't stay long and I looted the condiment bowl for sugar as we left.

Everyone who is released from prison in Kenya has to spend six days in police custody. That is their rule.

"Well, I'm free, aren't I? Let's just go."

"We can't do that. It's ok for you, but we've got to stay and work here and we have to go by their rules," Jill said.

We had to go to court again to get permission – another six days in a cell would be agony.

"Can Mr Johnson fly home to England tonight? Can he go home?" requested Nigel.

"Yes, no problem. He doesn't look like a threat to anyone. Yes, he can go home."

"One other thing, can you check if Mr Johnson can return in the future?" He looked down at paperwork, which he shuffled, and said, "Yes he can, there is no ban on Mr Johnson, he is free to return."

We rushed into the airport to collect my new temporary passport (at a cost of twenty quid) and checked in. I turned to go to departures, waving at them both.

"Oi, you've forgotten something," said Jill. I went back over and hugged her.

"Do you realise this is my last case? I'm retiring. Me and hubby have almost finished building a house in Mount Kenya."

"That's brilliant. I know the place well, it's my favourite place."

"Happy retirement," I said, and I pecked her cheek.

"Take care of yourself." She patted my back as we parted.

37. Scabies and Alzheimer's

During the lead up to my release I noticed a rash in between my fingers which seemed to get itchier by the day; with my track record with prison doctors, I thought I'd wait till I got home.

It was a locum covering for my doctor who was on holiday at the time. He told me what it was but I had a feeling it was more than just a heat rash. A week later, it spread up both arms; this time I saw my own doctor.

"I'm guessing you've been to Africa?"

I smiled, surprised by his reaction. "Yeh, I've just come back from Mombasa."

He held my hand inspecting it. "Yeh, I've been there, well I used to work there, I've seen this many times before. Scabies," he said. "You've got scabies; it's a long time since I've seen it but it's definitely scabies."

I was just happy that he knew his stuff. He gave me a pink ointment, which I covered myself in and it eventually got rid of the rash and sores, but it took two years to get rid of that crawling under the skin feeling.

When I phoned the surgery I found out Ann had been seeing the doctor for depression for the last six months. I arranged for the doctor to examine her at the house and he told me more or less what I already knew, but I knew there was more.

I managed to get her downstairs for the doctor's visit. I sat her in a chair, propped up by pillows and she was watching *Only Fools and Horses*. I told her the doctor was there to see her; she looked over as he approached her, and then looked back into the telly. I put a chair next to hers and the doctor sat down. He was in his forties; short and spoke with a lisp. He lifted his tan leather brief case onto his lap, pulled the zip across and rummaged about.

He looked up from the case. "She's got Alzheimer's." I snapped at him while Ann stayed glued to telly.

Ann completely ignored us, glued to the tv.

"Now let's not jump to conclusions, we need to run some tests first," he said, trying to calm me down.

"Tests, you don't need fucking tests, she's got fucking Alzheimer's and it's getting worse. Look, when I got home they said it was depression. It's not depression. She didn't even recognise me, she's forgotten how to look after herself, she doesn't even know when she needs the toilet, for fuck's sake."

I was getting irate, but I did calm down. I think he got the message.

"I understand she's been housebound for a while."

"Yeh, she likes staying upstairs, for some reason she seems happy up there."

"Why don't you want to go downstairs?" he tapped her on the arm, but it got no response.

"Mrs Johnson, can you hear me?"

"Why don't you like coming downstairs?"

Her gaze was on me, with the same blank expression as before, searching my face for an answer.

"Mrs Johnson, I need to examine you now." He unravelled the stethoscope from his bag and put it to each ear as he spoke. "Can you undo the top few buttons of your nightgown?" She did what he said, not taking her gaze from Del Boy. He moved the instrument around the top of her chest, listening each time as she took deep breaths.

"Can you lift it up at the back, right to your shoulders and lean forward please?"

I went over and helped her. Then he did the same examination on her back. He turned to me and unplugged the stethoscope from each ear. "Her lungs don't sound good, we'll need to get her in for some checks. How many does she smoke?"

"Twenty a day."

"She needs to cut down and you need to get her out of the house, get her exercising. How long has she been like this?"

"A couple of years … I think." He looked at me.

"I've been away, out of the country."

"Family? Any family been around?"

"Only David...her son."

I explained that he had learning difficulties and was visiting twice a week and not helping her situation at all. As the doctor left he told me he'd refer her to hospital so they could run a few tests, and advised me about Ann seeing a psychiatrist, which I agreed to.

I phoned the social worker and told him about David and his frequent visits, which they knew nothing about. I asked him to put a stop to the visits while I got things sorted and maybe keep them down to once a month.

A week later he turned up. A short bloke in his fifties with thinning curly ginger hair came to the house with a young woman assistant who he introduced as Phoebe and asked if it was alright for her to come in as well. She was a medical student and just stood back by the window and observed.

He started asking her all sorts of questions and although she was more talkative than she was before with the doctor, she wasn't giving any clues away. Dentures, she needs dentures, why can't she have dentures? Ann started to cry; that was enough.

"That's it, time to go." They both looked at each other as I said it. I walked to the door opened it and stood there waiting for them to leave.

"I know it's hard for you, but we are here for you and your wife."

"No thanks," and I slammed the door shut after them. I know they were trying to help but I didn't need their questions or their help, it was just upsetting Ann and it seemed they were making things worse.

I could see she was in bad physical shape but judging by the overall condition of the house I knew there was something else.

The results came back and I was right. Alzheimer's. Social ser-vices called me as well – offering me carers and respite; thank you but no thank you. I know I was stubborn but I knew that after what I had been through over the last two years, I was able to cope mentally and physically.

38. Drinking and Smoking

I was having a few drinks every day and kept a bottle of whisky in the hope it would relax me; I kept a bottle in the house, not for very long though. I'd stand with a glass and a fag on my front door step in the early hours, looking down at my street. The best time for this was four in the morning; the silence everywhere chilled me out.

Soon, I realised I was drinking two to three bottles a week; it was too much.

The booze started to make me feel groggy when I woke up and it seemed to sap all my energy in the end. I struggled to give Ann the round the clock attention she needed. I had to be on alert at all times and give her my full attention and so I gave up.

Like the drink, I'd always had this excessive streak about me; whatever I did, I went over the top, but only for a certain time. I would control it before it controlled me.

When I was younger I had a problem with eating. I loved to eat but wasn't happy with a chocolate bar, I'd wolf the packet down. I'd think nothing of buying a litre of ice cream and a tin of custard, destroying the lot in one go. I've always worked hard but I did reach twenty stone once, then realised I struggled at work and I became self-conscious about my appearance so I would diet, and I was lucky enough to lose weight quite quickly.

I knew the drink was making me ill. The combination of alcohol and unhealthy food made the physical and mental demands of looking after Ann 24/7 even tougher. A few mornings I would get up with severe pain in my legs and toes; I never saw a doctor so I never got a diagnosis but I knew it was my circulation, so it was time for action. I completely gave up alcohol and monitored how I felt eating certain foods. Bread was the worst, it gave me constant indigestion and I always felt tired and bloated so I never touched it. I lived on rice pudding made with skimmed milk, cooked and flavoured with a chopped banana and topped with low fat yoghurt. I also decided to eat lots of chicken salad and fruit and tinned fish every day, like sardines or mackerel, which are full of omega oils, and now I feel great.

The next problem I had was stopping her smoking. I don't know how that house was still standing. She'd light one and forget about it, leave it burning somewhere, then light another, leaving scorch marks everywhere.

Mentally, it was hard for me. She constantly demanded the cigarettes. I would tell her anything in the hope she would forget.

"Ok Ann, give me a chance to roll one," and then she would forget and five minutes later she'd ask again. I'd say the same thing, and so it went on for most of each day, and this went on for weeks.

One day she asked, and I gave the usual answer and she looked at me in total disbelief. "Come on, you can roll one faster than that." I couldn't stop laughing, her reply and expression was like the Ann of old and it took me by surprise.

"Hang on a minute, you're an expert, you've been smoking all your life, you know how to roll one faster than that." For a moment she realised she'd made me laugh and started laughing too, but then it got frustrating because she repeated this all day, so in the end I gave in to keep my sanity. I gave it to her and made sure I watched her smoke, then I took it off her and made sure the thing was put out.

She used to smoke twenty a day and slowly I cut them down and finally won the battle, and after that she would randomly ask for one every few weeks, but when she did, I changed the subject so she'd forget. That was a big challenge.

Ann smoked her last cigarette on 19th February 2003.

The one and only time I did call social services was for a wheelchair – I was turned down, their finances didn't stretch that far. They told me to try the Salvation Army – fuck that, I thought, so I struggled on without one, until I made my own. I found a plastic container in the road, it had four wheels attached and may have been used for a dustbin or something. I took it home and attached a deck chair to it, binding the legs tightly with rope. I used to help her down the stairs, sit her in it and wheel her across the living room to her spot in front of the telly. It made her giggle every time she went in it.

I was at the bottom of the garden one day when a friend shouted over.

He had relatives staying with him at the time and he told them about my struggle and my DIY wheelchair.

"Eh, they've got a spare wheelchair. They live up north but the next time they visit they're gunna bring for ya, ok?" And they did – I didn't use it much though.

The path from the house with ten steep steps was a problem and getting her weak frail frame down them and into the waiting chair was a nightmare. I didn't drive and the buses back then couldn't cope with wheelchairs so I would end up pushing her around the estate. In the end it became a military operation just to get her outside, and when we did, we got abuse from kids who followed us. So in the end I decided to keep her in the house.

I made sure she came down the stairs every day and we did eventually get a stairlift fitted, which made our lives a lot easier.

I dug another tonne of soil from the top tier just under the front room window, which made the plants around seem higher and screened it from the road. I paved a seating area and I'd bring Ann out to enjoy the sunshine.

Fifteen years back, the council put cheap single glazing in all the downstairs windows; I'd just as well leave the windows open, that's how crap they were. I not only could feel cold air blowing around the edge of the window but I could never get the rooms warm, so I decided to take action and double glaze them myself. I kept thick polythene sheets in my shed from a site I worked at a few years previously, cut them to size and taped them to the inside of the windows. I did go a bit mad with the Sellotape though. When I finished, no one could see in and I couldn't see out, which was fine because there was fuck all to see anyway.

The gas man called one day and made his checks; we didn't talk, he just got on with his job, read the meter, left and went next door.

"Eh, what's up with him next door then, your neighbour," he said to Glyn.

"Terry? What d'you mean?"

"The whole place is taped up with polythene, he's even stopped the air coming from the cold tap by taping the end of it."

Glyn didn't bother explaining the actions of the eccentric old fool next door, he just made a joke of it and laughed. Nothing wrong with Terry, he just loves his Sellotape, that's all. Me and my Sellotape were the talk of the estate and for Christmas that year from the neighbours, I unwrapped six rolls of it.

A bit extreme but it worked. I've got a digital clock in the lounge and it's got a built in thermometer; the polythene kept more heat in so I could turn the heating off saving more money.

I eventually paid the money back to South West Water in monthly instalments. It was a great feeling and I felt proud, making that last payment, knowing I had scraped by.

I was on benefits but was still able to pay my debt. I was determined to keep my bills to a minimum and use less water, well less of mine anyway. I found out my neighbours weren't on a meter so I bought two plastic dustbins and he would run his hosepipe over the fence and half fill them for me. I left one in the middle of the patio for the sun to warm up and another one near my back door and carried them upstairs and used them for baths.

Ann was unable to get in and out of the bath so I would strip wash her every morning and every night and carry the bins of water up the stairs. I made sure my daily shower was a quick one.

39. Hernia and Food Parcels

In the January I felt a pull at the base of my stomach like a strain; I wasn't sure what it was but the lump got bigger and more painful. I left it for a fortnight before seeing the doctor about a hernia that seemed to get bigger by the day.

I made a support and used a bolster pillow between my legs secured with a three-inch leather belt. Every twenty minutes I'd have to lie down and push the lump back in again.

My sister in Canada rang me and told me the danger – she used to be a nurse and she knew her stuff. "If that won't go back in you're going to kill yourself. I'll give you the money, go now and have the operation privately because you're not going to make it." I refused. Thanks ever so much but I'll be alright. I used to have to go down to the shop at six in the morning when it opened so no one could see me bent over hobbling around. It was crazy thinking back, what was I trying to prove. My neighbour Michael saw me coming back from the shops and could see I was in pain. I would only get a few paces forward and would stop, dropping the bags to the floor, the pain cutting through my groin as I stood in the street trying to push the lump back in. Give me that bag he said, marching over to me and he took the heavy bag and walked home with me. Since then his own health has deteriorated but I've never forgotten that day he helped me and now its my turn to help him by bringing his wheelie bins around to the front of his house on bin days.

I stubbornly struggled on refusing help, spending ninety days in agony until I finally had the operation. I still to this day don't know what I was trying to prove I felt I had a positive mental outlook on everything. I could cope with whatever life threw at me.

Looking after Ann was hard work, but I had a routine and knew I could do it on my own. I would bring her downstairs in the afternoon, she had a little walk around, then I got her climbing the stairs and I made sure she had protein and lots of fresh fruit in her diet.

I got up at two or three o'clock in the night – every night – to take her to the toilet, and if I didn't she'd mess the bed but would complain like a child when I got her up. "I don't need to go," she would say. The truth is, she had no control over her bodily functions so I would pre-empt this by waking her and taking her to the loo. I bound the toilet seat with layers of kitchen paper to make it more comfortable for her, and I'd sit her there for fifteen minutes or so but she would normally doze off again. I got her up at six to do it again, and afterwards, I would bring her down for breakfast and while she was awake, I took her to the loo every hour and a half. When she spoke she forgot what she wanted to say or I had to guess and maybe finish off her sentence for her.

"Where's my?"

"Food?"

"Yes"

"In front of you."

"Ah yeh."

"Can I have some toast?"

"In your left hand."

"Ah yeh," she said, realising she was holding it.

Sometimes she'd smile and laugh about it. The way I dealt with it all was humour, acting bloody stupid, turning things into a joke. When I took her to the toilet as often as I did we'd have banter. I'd start a phrase and let her fill the answer then I changed it.

"Sit down before I…"

"…knock you down?" she answered correctly.

"No, before I kiss you." She knew it wasn't right and she started laughing.

The furthest I walked was to the Co-op, three hundred yards down the road. I went in at Christmas and spoke to Laura.

"Where's the box? The Christmas box, you know tips…"

"No, they've stopped that, told us we can't do that anymore."

"Whaaat? Miserable bastards." I went back down a few days later and gave Laura a hundred quid.

"Here you are, Laura. Buy all the staff lottery tickets, Merry Christmas."

At the time, all the kids used to hang around outside in the street and my neighbour's kids were young at the time.

"No, I won't let my kids out there with that lot."

"Well, you'll need a bigger tv then."

"Yeh, I will when I win the lottery."

One year later I had saved up enough to buy them a fifty-inch plasma, which I did, and a seventeen thousand-litre swimming pool that filled their back garden. "There, that should keep them off the streets." They were all speechless.

Barbara would come over and take my shopping list – the things I couldn't get myself she would bring to me.

"Mr Johnson, you can have help you know, you don't have to struggle on your own." That's all I got from the doctors every time they called, they couldn't believe how I coped with no help from family.

"You can even have a nurse to stay the night to give you a rest." They visited quite regularly at first to see how I was coping and I would say the same thing every time.

They got used to my answer, "It's no problem, I'm ok," and as time went on they realised how bloody stubborn I was. The Health Visitor used to come over and look over the house and make sure I was ok.

"Sorry about the state of the kitchen," I said.

She looked at me in amazement. "Whaaat! It's cleaner than mine."

One early morning I looked out of my window and saw the back of a woman going down my steps. It was early morning and dark but I could make out from the streetlight near my house she had dark shoulder-length hair and a side-on view of her face told me she was in her thirties. I opened the door to get a better look and moved so quickly that I nearly tripped over the box that was there on my step. Reacting quickly, I hurdled it and raced down the steps with my slippers on. I was expecting her to turn left where the cars were parked but she took a right and followed a footpath then I heard an engine start and a car drive away.

Confused, I walked back to the house and opened the box. Tinned ham, luxury chocolate biscuits, expensive looking tea and coffee – all sorts of goodies. This happened every few months and I never did find out who it was for sure, but it may have been Social Services. I had from the start refused help of any kind and they could see I was – in their words – doing an incredible job of looking after Ann by myself. Nurses came to take blood and would report back to social services who were equally astonished at how I was coping on my own. So maybe it was them. Leaving anonymous gifts on my doorstep was maybe their way of helping a stubborn old bastard like me. The parcel always turned up between three and five o'clock in the morning so a shift worker, maybe a nurse. I'll never know, but if they read this then I would like to thank them for their kindness.

I was cutting hedges at the front of the house and went in to get my fags; as I came out a white council van pulled up and two middle-aged guys in smart suits got out and went a few doors down. As they went through the gate, I said, "Oi mate, she's gone out, back in about an hour's time."

I carried on clipping and they walked back towards me. "We're looking for a Mr Johnson, any ideas where he lives?"

I could see by his van he was council and the fact he didn't know my address meant he wasn't a debt collector, there was nothing to collect anyway.

"I may do. What the bloody hell has he done now?"

"Are you Mr Johnson?" he said, smiling.

"Yep."

"Well we're from Plymouth City Council, we've come about your nightly activities." I didn't have a clue. "It's been reported that you go out all hours of the night, three or four o'clock in the morning picking up litter with an old shopping bag."

Too much time spent on my doorstep, that was my problem. Between three and four after putting her back to bed I would stand there, fed up of seeing the same old bloody rubbish flying around, so I used to get out and clean the street.

"For Christ's sake, don't bend your back anymore. We've got something for you." The bloke beckoned me over to the van. "Look, take your pick." Every conceivable gadget for picking up rubbish was laid out. No bending down now. I chose a plastic and metal one with a trigger to grip with.

"Here you go, where do you want these?" He took out a box full of rubbish sacks, I nodded towards the front step and he placed them there for me.

"Thanks very much for all you do here, it's much appreciated."

"No problem," I said.

Just before they left the window came down. "Oh, by the way, how's your wife?"

"Fine thanks," and they drove away.

40. Breakfast at Gatwick

Once in a while I would have to go into town, so just as Ann got off to sleep, I would get the number nine bus into town. My visit was always timed and planned out so I would be back for when she woke up. After a restless night she seemed to sleep longer in the mornings and after breakfast she would sleep till lunch. I took full advantage of this time once and went out for breakfast.

The Plymouth to Gatwick flight took just under an hour and it left at half past six in the morning. The plane landed and I went straight into departures and found the nearest place for a full English breakfast. As I ordered, I recognised a bloke that was on my plane, he was in front of me in the queue.

I found a table and I was half-way through my food when the same bloke came over.

"You got through then?" he said, referring to the hold up getting into departures. This was his intro and he was desperate to tell me all about his holiday, where he was going and what he was doing.

So I put him out of his misery. "Where you off to then?"

"Florida," he said, with a wide smug grin on his face. He was meeting up with friends over there and went into detail about the hotel, Disneyland and other trips involving dolphins and the glades.

After a while the conversation ran dry and he seemed happy that I knew exactly where he was going and when he was fully satisfied he asked me, "So where are you off to then?"

"Plymouth."

"Plymouth?"

"Yeh, I'm gunna finish this and get the next plane home."

He stood quiet for a second, taking in what I'd just told him. "Yeh, I only came here for the breakfast."

He grinned at me. "You flew here from Plymouth just for breakfast?"

"Yeh."

I carried on eating as he turned to his family.

"Aye Michael, come here." The rest of the family followed, they sensed excitement in his voice and gathered around my table. "Have a guess where this man's going?" Without giving them a chance he answered, "He's going back to Plymouth. He only came here for breakfast." He started to laugh and the others looked on in disbelief and joined in. "How fucking mad is that?" Excited by it all, he clapped his hands together. "Right, want do you want to drink?"

"No, no it's ok."

"Let me buy you a drink, come on, have a whisky with me." This man was not listening to no.

"Ok, I'll have a Jameson's".

He turned to his brother who already had his wallet open and was walking back to the bar.

"Michael, get this man a Jameson's, make it a double."

They thought that was great but however mad my trip seemed it was just what I needed.

I got back four hours later, and Ann was just beginning to stir. I had gotten back just in time. I know a day return to Gatwick just for breakfast sounds eccentric but I think I just wanted to kid myself I was going on holiday away from 65, James Gardens – I guess I really did need a break.

It was 2009 before I finally conceded and took social services up on their offer of looking after Ann. This was my first rest in years, a long time without a break, and it was only when I got on that plane again that I realised how stressful my situation had been. I had to go back to Kenya, but this time I would not be coming home again with drugs – I can safely say I learnt the hard way where that was concerned. No, there was only one place I needed to go and that was back there. I booked Ann into a nurse-staffed place for two weeks.

The buzz of flying seemed to tap into my emotions again, bringing me back to life. I had all the old feelings of excitement back again. I packed my case a week before, bought some new clothes and couldn't wait, but it wasn't until the plane left the runway that I expressed my true emotions. As it took off I could feel myself getting weaker and weaker, I started to fight back – get a grip, Terry, I said to myself – but I couldn't control it, I failed as tears welled up in my eyes, blurring my vision before rolling down my cheeks. I bent my head lower, shielding my hand to my face, trying to hide them. If someone had spoken to me I would have totally broken down. I slowly recovered my composure and ten minutes later I was fine. On the second trip I told myself it wouldn't happen again but at the same moment the plane left the runway the same thing happened again.

I wanted to go and see if there was any sign of the grave but in the end I decided against it.

I also wanted to go back to the Mambo crocodile farm. There are about 10,000 crocodiles and the place looks like it started off as one big quarry. Over the years they've built it up with its own irrigation system so it looks like a really green lush oasis. Lots of steps and pathways snake around into bars and restaurants with crocodiles at different stages of life. As well as watch them you can taste them by eating crocodile and chips in the Mambo Disco in the evening. I didn't stay there long and in the taxi on the way back I did see something strange. We were going about forty or fifty miles an hour. As trees flashed past, I saw through them, about twenty lads in a line with their hands tied behind their backs. I didn't say anything to the driver and I don't suppose he even noticed but I had experienced enough in Kenya by this stage not to be surprised.

It was a night flight home and the nurse suggested it would be best if I went home, got some sleep and took her the next day. I was home for three hours and the phone rang and it was bad news. "Mr Johnson, your wife has been taken to hospital, she's an emergency."

I turned up and the doctor asked how she'd got into that state. I told him where I'd been and this was the first time I'd seen her in two weeks.

He took me aside and explained that her body had completely shut down and the noise I could hear was from the machine; he pointed to the one she was connected to, telling us that she had far too much carbon dioxide in her blood. That was at four in the afternoon and I stayed, holding her hand for the next twelve hours. I asked for a drink of water, which never arrived, so I went and got one. The doctor met me in the corridor.

"You realise, Mr Johnson, that your wife is seriously ill, it's very unlikely she'll make it, she's not responding." I nodded back, understanding the situation fully.

I sat in the corridor holding my cup in a trance when another doctor came over. "I'm very sorry Mr Johnson, very sorry but there's no hope for your wife, she is very weak, you've done a great job looking after her." So that was two doctors in the space of half an hour, both telling me my wife was going to die.

The nurse told me to go home and get some rest, and that's what I did, but not for long. Something told me to go back. She'd been moved to a ward upstairs – there was nothing else they could do for her.

I held her hand all the time, chatting to her, swearing as well trying to get her to react, waiting for a 'Terry, do you have to use language like that' kind of response.

"Fucking hell Ann, don't leave me like this, don't die now, for fuck's sake." Then it happened. She opened her eyes and spoke.

"I love you," she said and then closed them again. Five minutes later, she sat up straight and looked around the ward as if nothing had happened. "He's nice." I thought she was bloody delirious or dreaming as I followed her eyes to a young handsome dark-haired doctor stood behind a desk.

Soon after, we were talking normally, just like the old Ann. The doctors were amazed, they couldn't understand how she made a recovery as quick as she did.

"We don't use the word 'miracle' here very often but what's happened to your wife is truly amazing," the doctor said. They kept her in for a few extra days so I could rest.

41. Kettle Lady

A year later, and I was ready for my second respite and booked myself back to Kenya. I did my usual calendar countdown and couldn't wait. Escaping the house for the second time in eight years was a dream that was getting closer.

I started packing two months before my holiday; everything was ironed and hung around the room and I bought a few short-sleeved shirts to wear in the evening.

At first I was worried about leaving Ann on her own again because of what happened, but doctors explained it was no one's fault and could have so easily happened even if I was looking after her. I knew how great the staff were and knew she would be taken care of, so I came to the decision that I needed a break and there was only one place to go.

The night flight from Heathrow landed at Nairobi at 6.30 in the morning where I would get the connecting flight to Mombasa.

I went through passport control and this is where my rest/holiday ended before it started. The guy took my passport and scanned it. Keeping hold of my passport I could see him reading, checking a list in front of him. Then he told me to wait while he spoke to his colleague and they both came back over and told me to follow them into a staff door.

"What's going on?" They didn't answer. In fact they didn't speak to me at all until they summoned another guy who told me.

"You are not allowed into Kenya." When I questioned him he wouldn't give a reason. Obviously I knew the reason but explained I had been allowed back into the country last year and told him what the judge had said years ago. 'Mr Johnson appears to be no further threat and is allowed back into Kenya at any time in the future.' This guy wasn't really listening.

"You want money like last time? Yeh, ok, how much?"

He told me the decision was made by his boss.

"I want a reason why you chose this time and not before to refuse me.

"That bloke you spoke to, your boss, I want to speak to him now. If you think I'm a threat, check my bags and check them when I go home."

I was tired and getting irritated by the minute. "For god's sake, I've spent £800 on this holiday which has taken me a long time to save for – I look after my wife 24/7 and need this holiday." I offered money again. "How much does your boss want?"

The guy said he would speak to his boss but never came back to me for money, which was strange as I knew from the last time I was there, how desperate they were.

I was escorted to departures by another guard whose job it was to make sure I got on the plane.

I wandered around duty free with this guy in tow, looking for cigarettes. I'd come this far so I was definitely going to stock up. As I left the till I saw the Kettle Lady. The same person that had arrested me years before; she walked towards me oblivious at first until I stepped in front of her.

"Hello, remember me?"

I sat with the very friendly Kettle Lady and we chatted. I told her my situation, which she could do nothing about but explained about the updated technology they were using to trace passports. That explained why I was able to visit the year before. We sat reminiscing about my arrest.

"I was convinced that we had the wrong person," she said.

"You just seemed unnaturally calm."

"Yeh, had a lot on my mind." I didn't go into detail about my family I'd buried forty hours before. It was that calmness that stayed with me until I got to remand when everything changed and I was acting and living off my wits 24/7.

"Here." I took her hand, squashing a two thousand bob note into it; she gave me a 'what's that for?' sort of look.

"The kettle, remember the kettle?" Again she looked at me as if I was insane but clearly wasn't going to hand it back.

I knew she wouldn't buy a kettle but I'd kept my promise and I could tell by her reaction she thought it was strange. A promise fulfilled by a stranger she arrested years ago was bizarre, but that's me.

"You've come all the way here and you've got to go all the way back. That must have cost you a lot of money." The guard who was with me all along decided to speak now, not sure if he took offence at being left out of the earlier donation but he was gloating at my situation.

I flipped. "You're having a laugh at my expense, are you?"

He just grinned. "What do you know about me, mmm? I'm white, I'm old, is that it? I've spent sixteen months in your prison, is that correct?"

He didn't answer. "Shouldn't that send alarm bells ringing through your fucking stupid head? I know all about you. I know what you eat. I know where you live. I know exactly what you all do here. I know the system to this place. I know everything. What do you know about me?"

Nothing. The Kettle Lady diffused the situation by standing between us both and told him she would take over from here.

"Come on, I'll take you back over to the Immigration Office before you get into any more trouble. Then I need to make sure you get on this plane."

Prevented from entering the country even though the judge agreed with Nigel and Jill that I could, my African dream was finally over.

42. The Best Scam of All

Someone once asked me what I loved about Kenya. I can't remember who it was but I remember my answer. The watu – the people. They are an amazing, resilient race. They are survivors and they are akili sana – very clever.

Although I would have worked on a Safari, I never once went on one as a tourist. Maybe it's a big distraction from the real wonders of Kenya – the watu.

The bad bits of my experience in Kenya took a while to get over. I kept having the same nightmares over and over, particularly about the grave, those bodies and even about that fucking flying cat, but the more I thought, the more I pieced together something that is obvious to me now but wasn't at the time.

Rewind back to the day at the airport when my girlfriend's neighbour came over. He'd seen me a few times, swimming with my son. His mood that day was buoyant and all he wanted to do was talk. How long I was staying for, where I was going, that sort of thing. News of births and deaths spread quickly around villages, especially when it involves a mzungu and a suicide. I find it hard to believe he didn't know, if he did, I don't think he would have acted the way he did – at best he would have avoided me.

Thinking back to when I met her in Mombasa, it was few years after we first met. I noticed the baby's colour. My girlfriend was from the northern tribe, very dark almost jet black – the baby was lighter and would have expected him to be much darker. My son looked really healthy, well fed, she on the other hand looked scrawny thin in her scruffy clothes. They didn't look right together. I replayed our meetings over and over in my mind and there was a certain awkwardness between them and the way they interacted with each other. It wasn't natural and seemed forced.

We'd spend time away, just the two of us, and I'd suggest picking the boy up but she sometimes made excuses, preferring to spend time on our own, which I'd thought nothing out the ordinary, she just needed a bit of time for herself I guess but it always away from the village, sometimes with the boy, sometimes without. That should have seemed strange to me but I never gave it a second thought. An African with a mzungu boyfriend and son would want to show me off like a trophy, or even drag me into Mombasa to spend my money but this never happened. My girlfriend spoke very good English but my son on the other hand didn't speak a word. At some early stage, a Kenyan woman with a mzungo baby would be thinking of a new life in England and would have encouraged my son to learn English, after all I was their ticket to England and a new life.

I'd seen and experienced all sorts of scams from walking the backstreets 'poking my nose in' to my time spent in prison. Corruption plays a big part in Kenyan life, it is in some cases survival of the fittest, not just in body but the mind too and it seems they go to any extreme to deceive and con in order to survive. This I found out to be true at my own cost.

The Baby Scam was quite an elaborate one and here's how it works. My friend the Landlord dreamt this one up. Sharon was twenty, not married and no kids, which in Kenyan terms, was unusual. Most girls marry and have kids as young as fifteen so the fact she was twenty and still waiting to be picked or overlooked was a factor in all this. It was him who introduced us with a clear intention – to make some cash.

First, he coached her on his plan and knew we hadn't seen each other for a few years and knew I contacted her through a PO box. I have no doubt she wasn't even from this village, her darker skin should have given that away, and he set her up in one of his empty houses whenever I visited.

The next part was borrowing a child so she could play the part of a mother to my child. After getting over the shock of being a dad again, I was ready, poised to face up to my responsibility and although I couldn't be there full time for the kid, I made sure I paid his mum enough money each month to make his life a little bit easier.

The Landlord just thought I was an old tourist who he could rinse money out of, but it wasn't until he found out from the beach boys that this harmless old tourist was in fact the drug dealer that they'd mentioned before and so the Landlord made the connection.

I was always a small time player but he wasn't to know this. Thinking the worst, the Landlord started to panic, he didn't want this backfiring on him. If I was involved in drugs he couldn't be sure who and what other stuff I was into and was desperate to keep his scam a secret. I wouldn't be best pleased if I found out the way in which he was scamming me. So he had to get rid of me before I discovered the whole charade.

Knowing when I would turn up he planned that day to send the girl away from the village, to meet me himself and tell me they both had died, that way I would have no reason to keep returning to the village and he was rid of me.

When he showed me the graves, he didn't expect me to dig them up, when I did, he knew it was somebody else's and left me to it.

That random grave he chose, the one that I dug up and re-buried belonged to somebody else. I plastered my hands with someone's decomposed limbs and when I got to the airport they had my description and were waiting for me, again thanks to my friend; The Landlord.

Now that's what I call a scam.

I had, throughout my Kenyan experience, gotten to know all the scams and how astute and desperate people over there could be in order to survive. It's only now looking back that I realised that this prison didn't want me there in the first place. A foreigner in a Kenyan prison would bring unwanted attention from outside officials and human rights and all they wanted was to be left alone to run their prison by their own rules. That's why I was put in

Segregation, kept away from the mainstream, not for my own safety, because I was still holed up with rapists and robbers it was more to do with hiding things from me, however that didn't work because I still got to see corruption and brutality on a daily basis.

It's strange how much luck one person can have before it changes. Luck started my story – winning 'Spot the Ball' changed my life. It was only seven and half grand but I wouldn't have got to Kenya without it. If Ann had her way, we wouldn't have left the country and our house would be full of gadgets and household items that never left their boxes. Money wasted. Luck followed me and saw me through my 'poking my nose in' situations and many of my drug smuggling scenarios.

How has my experience changed or affected me? Many have asked. Kenya has given me an inner strength of mind that I never knew existed, a strength that is with me today. I have experienced and seen first hand the real Kenya, the poverty, the corruption.

No one in this country can honestly claim to know what poverty is really like, hard conditions yes, but not the same as I saw over there. A life without fresh running water and places where stinking raw sewage spews out between the houses onto the streets where the kids play. It's another world and not a nice one.

Basic food, like bread, eggs and milk, food we take for granted is a luxury over there. No one starves here like they do there.

It's made me realise what we have in this country, like the NHS; if we're sick we go to the doctors – good, qualified ones – and they treat us or get us referred to hospital as easy as that, ok maybe a waiting list to moan about but you will be treated. If you're ill in Kenya, unless you have money, you carry on being ill, suffering – no one is going to help and life becomes even tougher.

I used to take for granted everything we have in this country but with my insight, my African insight, I now make an extra effort to appreciate the simple things like doing my bit around the house, conserving energy and I never waste water. I use and if needs be, reuse the same water for certain things like collecting rainwater in those water butts. In the end that gave me a bloody hernia, a bit extreme, but I felt humbled by my experience and compelled to do my bit.

I survived the hardship of an African prison at the age of sixty and didn't know at that time that I was actually being groomed, preparing me for what lay ahead, the next step in my life as a full time carer, a different type of prisoner in a house that most of the time feels like a prison. Eleven years on and that same strength and verve for life is still with me today, propelling me along, keeping me going 24/7 without the help of family. It's just the two of us and we have a finely tuned routine that works for us both.

Seeing Ann that first day back of course, I felt guilty but I'd been so unhappy for years, so when the opportunity came up, I left to chase my dream and I don't regret one minute, it was all meant to be as far as I'm concerned.

I actually feel enriched by it all, privileged that I got to see the things I did, the good, the bad and horrific. If I knew I was going to die tomorrow I'd feel content knowing that my Kenyan experience meant that Terry Johnson had lived, and experienced more in five years than most people would ever see in their entire lives.

I hadn't intended to break the law smuggling drugs, it was a means to an end and I didn't want my dream to end, so if that meant taking more risks, then so be it, but I paid for it in the end.

The arresting officer was right; African prison was hard for an old bloke like me. I wasn't beaten and abused but the conditions, the food and the whole segregation way of life took its toll and at one point I thought I would die there.

The thing that kept me going, and what keeps me going to this day looking after Ann, is humour. The ability to forget the hardship of a situation and convert it to laughter is what got me through it all and it's what gets me through caring for someone whose body and mind don't work, someone who is totally reliant on me 24/7. Two breaks in eight years is testament to that.

Asante Sana. Thank you very much.

Po Box 4156
Nairobi

Dear Mr Johnson,

I anticipate you have good health.
I write this letter with euphoria.

Thank you for your generosity. I was released
from Kamiti on 12/04/2003.

I was bewildered. I was ordered to see the Officer
in Charge. He gave me your correspondence.
Astounding! you remembered me one year later.

The money you sent, I acquired a bicycle to
travel now look for work. I do not want to go
back to prison.

From *Jacob* (Thesaurus)

03:00hrs. Sunday 16th December 2012

I got Ann up for her well practised trip to the loo.
I lifted her out of bed to stand but her legs gave
way, buckling from underneath her.

I tried holding her up but her weak body had
other ideas as I battled with her, urging her to
stand for her self but it was no good.

Her breathing was erratic and noisy. I reached
into a pocket for my mobile and rang for an
ambulance.

At the hospital nurses took charge connecting
her to a BiPAP machine fitting a mask over her
mouth. It works by clearing airways with oxygen
and that's how she spent the rest of the night and
morning. I sat beside her holding her hand as it
monitored levels of carbon dioxide in her
system. The number displayed fluctuated and at
one stage it looked like she was on the mend
again only for her number to rapidly decrease.

"Ann, can you hear me?" the nurse said tapping
her arm.

She slowly reacted with a nod.

"Do you have a pain" unable to lift the mask she
mumbled through it.

"Yes he's with me" .

Those were her last words.

11:00am. Ann passed away in hospital.

17042932R00132

Made in the USA
Charleston, SC
24 January 2013